Check out the photo of my current studio. It's been 16 years since coming to Tokyo, and during that time I've moved six times. This is my fifth studio, and also the first time we've arranged the desks to face one another, cafeteria style. Though it's kind of annoying to have to see everybody else's faces so often, my assistants and I are still getting work done. Also, the short story collection that I'm releasing in Japan along with this sixth volume of *Toriko* features a photo of my first studio. It was in a really run-down apartment... So even though I get to draw manga in a posh studio now, I can never shake the memory of that old place. (And for those of you who are still counting, my current weight is...70 kg!! Hmm... No change...)

–Mitsutoshi Shimabukuro, 2009

Mitsutoshi Shimabukuro made his debut in **Weekly Shonen Jump** in 1996. He is best known for **Seikimatsu Leader Den Takeshi!** for which he won the 46th Shogakukan Manga Award for children's manga in 2001. His current series, **Toriko**, began serialization in Japan in 2008.

TORIKO VOL. 6
SHONEN JUMP Manga Edition

STORY AND ART BY **MITSUTOSHI SHIMABUKURO**

Translation/Christine Dashiell
Adaptation/Hope Donovan
Touch-Up Art & Lettering/Maui Girl
Design/Sam Elzway
Editor/Alexis Kirsch

Printed in Canada

Published by VIZ Media, LLC
P.O. Box 77010
San Francisco, CA 94107

10 9 8 7 6 5 4 3
First printing, September 2011
Third printing, August 2019

TORIKO
Story and Art by
Mitsutoshi
Shimabukuro
6
TEN-FOLD!!

TORIKO
THE ULTIMATE GOURMET HUNTER WHO'S ON A NEVER-ENDING QUEST TO FIND AND SCARF UP THE RAREST FOODS ON EARTH! HE FIGHTS WITH A KNIFE (HIS FIST), A FORK (HIS FIST), AND SPIKED PUNCH (ALSO HIS FISTS).

WHAT'S FOR DINNER

●KOMATSU
IGO HOTEL CHEF AND TORIKO'S #1 FAN

●COCO
ONE OF THE FOUR KINGS, THOUGH HE ALSO IS A FORTUNE-TELLER. SPECIAL ABILITY: POISON FLOWS IN HIS VEINS.

●SUNNY
ANOTHER OF THE FOUR KINGS. SENSORS IN HIS LONG HAIR ENABLE HIM TO "TASTE" THE WORLD. OBSESSED WITH ALL THAT IS BEAUTIFUL.

TERRY CLOTH●
OFFSPRING OF THE MOST AMAZING WOLF TO EVER EXIST.

●RIN
AN IGO ANIMAL TRAINER WITH THE POWER OF SMELL AT HER DISPOSAL. SHE'S SUNNY'S LITTLE SISTER.

IT'S THE AGE OF GOURMET! KOMATSU, THE HEAD CHEF AT THE HOTEL OWNED BY THE IGO (INTERNATIONAL GOURMET ORGANIZATION), BECAME FAST FRIENDS WITH THE LEGENDARY GOURMET HUNTER TORIKO WHILE GATOR HUNTING. NOW KOMATSU ACCOMPANIES TORIKO ON HIS LIFELONG QUEST TO CREATE THE PERFECT FULL-COURSE MEAL.

ONE DAY, HE AND TORIKO ENCOUNTERED A GT ROBOT, A MACHINE DISPATCHED BY THE IGO'S RIVAL ORGANIZATION, GOURMET CORP. SENSING A FOUL PLOT AFOOT, THE IGO MADE AN EMERGENCY SUMMONS OF THE FOUR KINGS--THE TOP GOURMET HUNTERS IN THE WORLD. THEY ASKED THE FOUR KINGS TO TAKE ON GOURMET CORP.'S GT ROBOTS IN AN ULTIMATE SHOWDOWN OVER THE ANCIENT REGAL MAMMOTH!

SO TORIKO, ALONG WITH SUNNY, KOMATSU, RIN AND TERRY, COMMENCED A HARROWING JOURNEY TOWARD THE REGAL HIGHLANDS OF REGAL ISLE, HOME OF THE REGAL MAMMOTH. IT SEEMED GT ROBOTS HAD GOTTEN THERE FIRST, LEAVING TORIKO AND CO. TO DEAL WITH A LIVID MAMMOTH AND AN ENRAGED NEST OF FEROCIOUS HEAVY CLIFFS! FORTUNATELY, COCO SHOWED UP TO SAVE THE DAY. AS HE RAN INTERFERENCE, COCO WATCHED TORIKO'S GROUP GET SUCKED UP INTO THE MAMMOTH THROUGH ITS TRUNK. THE LAST THING HE SAW AS THEY WENT WAS A SHADOW OF DEATH HANGING OVER THEM...

NOW INSIDE THE MAMMOTH, SUNNY IS ABOUT TO TAKE ON ANOTHER GT ROBOT, WHILE TORIKO AND THE OTHERS PRESS ON IN SEARCH OF THE PRIZED JEWEL MEAT...

●STARJUN
VICE-CHEF

●GT ROBOT
THE GOURMET CORP.'S NEWEST ROBOT

Contents

GOURMET 44: COCO MEANS BUSINESS!!

TORIKO

SKIF
F
PLUP
PLIP PLUP
WOOOOOOO
HNNNGH
HNNNGH
RAAWR

PYOOOM

SKIID DD
DSH
HRNFF
HAAAHN
...
WHAT REFLEXES ...

A RELIC OF ANTIQUITY, THE ALMIGHTY BATTLE WOLF.
ACCORDING TO OUR HEAD CHEF...
I NEVER WOULD HAVE THOUGHT TO LAY EYES UPON ONE IN THE HUMAN WORLD.
THOUGH MERELY AN INFANT, YOUR AGILITY IS NO LESS THAN I'D EXPECT.
BATTLE WOLVES...

...YOUR KIND STILL RUNS WILD IN SOME CORNERS OF THE GOURMET WORLD.

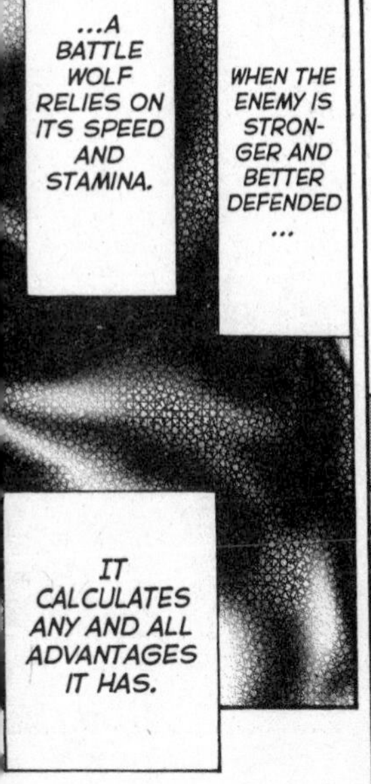

TO COMPEN-SATE, ALMOST ALL OF A LION'S MEALS COME FROM SIMPLY STEALING MEAT FROM THE HYENAS THAT BROUGHT IT DOWN.
THEY HAVE DISCOVERED THAT TO BE THE MOST EFFICIENT MEANS OF FILLING THEIR BELLIES.

EVEN LIONS, THE KINGS OF THE JUNGLE, IF LEFT TO HUNT ALONE, WILL MORE THAN LIKELY FAIL.
AND EVEN IN A PACK, THEIR CHANCE OF SUCCESS IS ONLY 20 TO 30 PERCENT.

AT THE MOMENT, TERRY'S CHANCES OF VICTORY WERE CLOSE TO ZERO.
SO TERRY KEPT HIS DISTANCE.

HE WAS FAR ENOUGH AWAY TO DODGE SUDDEN ATTACKS.
FIRST AND FOREMOST, THAT DIMINISHED THE ODDS OF HIM BECOMING MORTALLY WOUNDED.
HE JUST HAD TO WAIT FOR HIS ENEMY TO LEAVE HIMSELF OPEN.
SPEED AND STAMINA WERE ALL HE HAD TO WORK WITH.
SO LONG AS HE PAID CLOSE ATTENTION, HE COULD WIN THE MATCH...
...BY TURNING IT INTO AN ENDURANCE CONTEST.

HOW-EVER...
HMM... I DON'T SEE ANY OPENINGS.
YOU PAY CLOSE ATTENTION.
IN THAT CASE...
THE TWO PARTIES HAD DIFFER-ENT GOALS IN MIND.

I HAVEN'T TIME TO WASTE ON AN ENDURANCE TEST.
SHUF
IF YOU WILL NOT COME AT ME, I'LL BE MOVING ON.

TERRY KNEW HE HAD TO HALT THIS ENEMY, EVEN AT THE COST OF HIS OWN LIFE.
...!
BUT STARJUN COULDN'T HAVE CARED LESS ABOUT TERRY.

GRROAR
I LEAVE HE REST O YOU...

...

OBASAURUS!
GRARBLAAR
SKF
SKF
!!
GRAAWR
F
RRRRAR

GLUG
GLUG
HERE WE GO.
HIS TASTE ENSORS MUST BE OCATED ...
FWSH
HOLD IT RIGHT THERE, YOU HALF-OUNCE OF DUNG!!
B-TUM B-TUM B-TUM
... RIGHT THERE!
HAAAH ...
SLRRRP
CH

PEELER SHOT !!
KTING
TINKL
TCH!
GUESS MY BLADE WASN'T STRONG ENOUGH.
TWANG
SH !
SHOT!!!
OH N--!

WHOA!!
STUPID MOVE!!
PWA
EAT THIS!!
VWEEE
NOW'S MY CHANCE!!
RIFLE!!!
PYEW
KO OM
BOO
GWAH!!
SPOO

HRN ...
THUDD
HYAAAAH!!
KRSSSH!
GAHAH!!
NYOOM

WHAT DID YOU SQUIRT INTO MY MOUTH?

THIS SIGNAL TELLS ME THAT THE TASTE TRANSMISSION'S BEEN INTERRUPTED. FROM THE COMPONENT ANALYSIS, IT'S...

POISON!

YOU SMUG LITTLE WORM...!

YOUR DIRTY TRICKS ARE NOTHING BUT CHILD'S PLAY AGAINST A GT ROBOT!!

SMUSH

GUH...

SMUSH

HUH?

RIGHT HERE. YEAH, THAT'S GOOD.

THIS IS...

...A GREAT LOCATION.

IT'S FAR AWAY ENOUGH FROM THE MAMMOTH...

...AND NOW THAT THE HEAVY CLIFFS HAVE FLED...

...I CAN FINALLY FIGHT LIKE I MEAN BUSINESS. AND NOBODY...

WOOO

WOOOOOOOOO
NOBODY...
...DARES APPROACH ME.
--!

AAAAAA

I MUST HAVE CUT OFF THE CIRCULATION TO YOUR BRAIN. I'M A GT ROBOT. THE NEWEST MODEL!

I'VE SWUM THE POISON TIDE. VENOMS DON'T WORK ON ME.

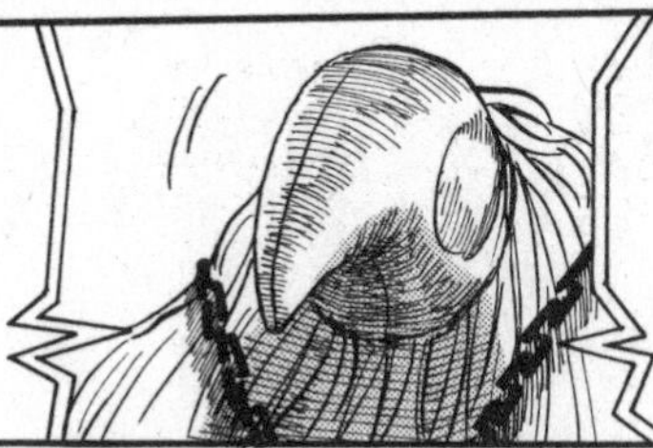

THE CURRENT OF DEATH KNOWN AS THE POISON TIDE, HUH? I LOVE THAT PLACE... HEY, I KNOW!

LET'S TEST WHICH IS MORE TOXIC--THE POISON TIDE... OR *ME!*

POISON HELL!!

TORIKO

GOURMET CHECKLIST

Vol. 029

TORIKO BURGER

(A TORIKO SIGNATURE ITEM)

CAPTURE LEVEL: IF YOU ADD UP CAPTURE LEVELS OF THE INGREDIENTS...OVER 40?!

HABITAT: WHEREVER TORIKO MAKES IT

LENGTH: ---

HEIGHT: ABOUT 70 CM

WEIGHT: 3 KG

PRICE: DEPENDS ON THE INGREDIENTS, BUT A RESTAURANT WOULD PROBABLY CHARGE 8500 YEN.

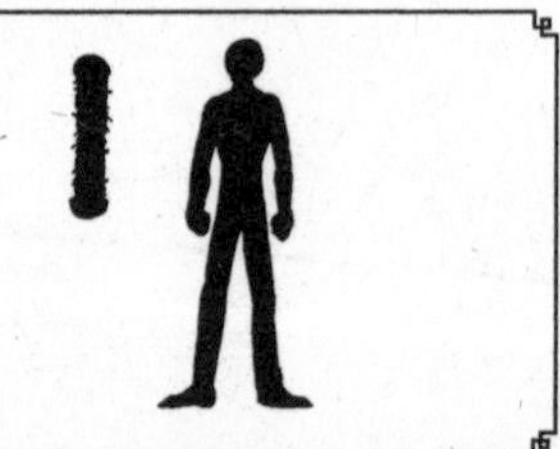

SCALE

WHAT'S BETTER THAN EATING YOUR FAVORITE THINGS? EATING THEM ALL TOGETHER! THAT'S THE PHILOSOPHY BEHIND THE TORIKO BURGER. BECAUSE TORIKO LIKES SO MANY FOODS, THE COMPOSITION OF THE SANDWICH VARIES EACH TIME HE MAKES IT, BUT ONE THING IS CONSTANT: ALL THE INGREDIENTS ARE HIGH-PRICED AND SUPER RARE! APPARENTLY, THE BIGGEST BURGER CHAINS OUT THERE HAVE ASKED TORIKO TO ENDORSE SIMILAR BURGERS ON THEIR MENU, BUT HE HASN'T SHOWN ANY INTEREST IN DOING SO.

GOURMET 45: AQUA REGIA!!

POISON HELL!!
--!!
SHOOOO
SSS

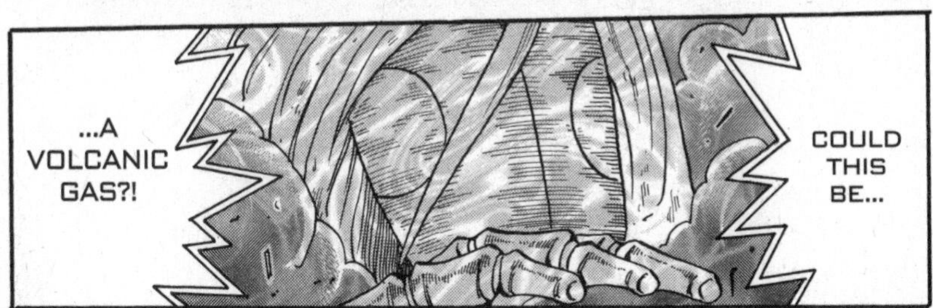

AN ELEMENT FOUND IN VOLCANOS AND NATURAL HOT SPRINGS. JUST THE PRESENCE OF .1% (1000 PPM) IN A SOLUTION CAN KILL AN ADULT HUMAN. AT A HIGH ENOUGH CONCENTRATION, HYDROGEN SULFIDE IS CAPABLE OF CORRODING METAL.

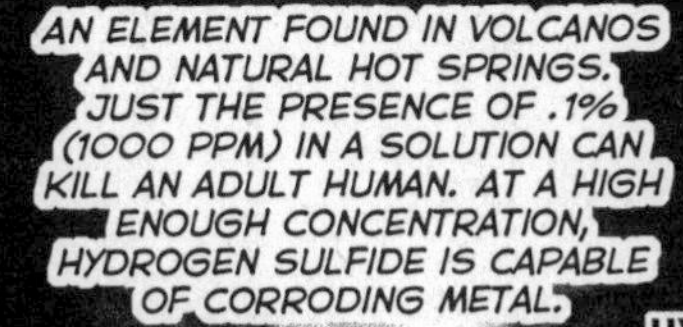

HYDROGEN SULFIDE

BY BREAKING DOWN THE WASTE PRODUCTS IN HIS BODY, COCO MIXED UP A HYDROGEN SULFIDE, WHICH HE THEN SPRAYED FROM HIS BODY.

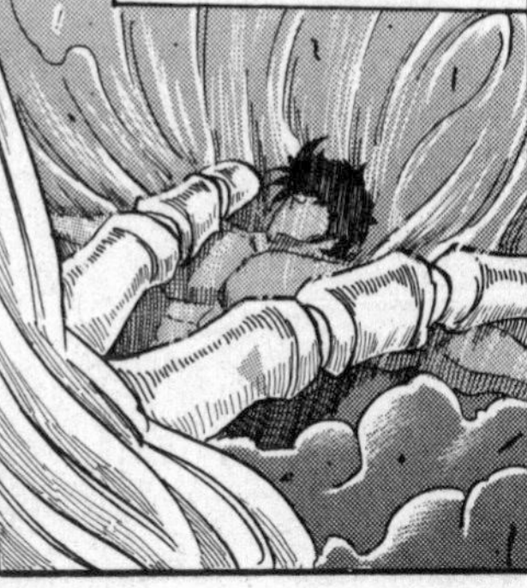

TOO BAD FOR YOU...

...THAT A GT ROBOT'S VERY PURPOSE IS TO TRAVEL TO PLACES HUMANS CANNOT.

THAT MEANS PLACES LIKE THE DEEP OCEAN, OR UNDERGROUND CAVES SATURATED WITH TOXIC FUMES...OR EVEN THE MOUTH OF AN ERUPTING VOLCANO.

WITH THESE CORROSION-PROOF BODIES MADE OF TITANIUM ALLOY, EVEN THE MOST CONCENTRATED GAS IS INEFFECTIVE.

IF THAT WAS YOUR FINAL ATTACK...

...THEN IT LOOKS LIKE YOU'RE ABOUT TO DIE...

...COCO OF THE FOUR KINGS!

ALL POINTS TAKEN.

BUT...WHAT IF I COULD PRODUCE AN EVEN STRONGER POISON THAN HYDROGEN SULFIDE?

ONE THAT WOULD MELT YOU RIGHT WHERE YOU STAND.

THIS SMOKE IS FLAMMABLE, I CAN TELL.
YOU'RE TRYING TO GET ME TO OPEN FIRE AND SET IT OFF, AREN'T YOU?
AM I RIGHT?
...
HMPH, DON'T TRY TO BLUFF.
IT'S OBVIOUS YOU'RE GRASPING AT STRAWS.
WUFF
I'M FEELING GENEROUS. I'LL BE A NICE GUY AND GRANT YOUR WISH.
NOT LIKE IT'LL HAVE ANY EFFECT ON ME.
AT LEAST IF I BLAST AWAY THE SMOKE I'LL GET A GOOD LOOK AT YOUR FACE WHEN YOU DIE!!
DWAAP
FOOM
POISON SHIELD !!

THOO
BRRUUM

BOOOOOOOM
HA!!! I AM INDE-STRUCTI-BLE!!
I BLEW MYSELF UP AND LOOK-- NO DAMAGE !!
DO YOU GET IT YET, POISON MAN?
SNPP

HUFF
HUFF
LOOKS LIKE YOU TOOK MORE DAMAGE THAN ME. SERVES YOU RIGHT.
THOUGH IT'S QUITE IMPRES-SIVE YOU CAN STILL BREATHE AFTER SUCH AN EXPLOSION. BUT EITHER WAY...
PWAAP
I'M ALL OUT OF POISON.
ALL I CAN DO NOW...IS HAVE FAITH IN THE AMOUNT I USED EARLIER.
THE ONE WITH THE SHADOW OF DEATH HANGING OVER HIM...
VWEEE
...TURNED OUT TO BE YOU, BUDDY.

SO LONG.
BJOOOM
SIZZ
ZRT
BRUMM
KTING
!

SZZZZ
SZZZZ
WOOOOO
HMM ...?
...?
I MISS-ED?
AT POINT BLANK RANGE?
WHAT'S THE MATTER?
I THOUGHT THAT BODY WAS STATE-OF-THE-ART.
SHUT UP!!
KW
KTATAT
THWUMP
OOP
HWUH?!

SWOO
HRNGH
...
WHAT'S... HAPPEN-ING...?
SWOO

PHEW
...
LOOKS LIKE...

...I MANAGED TO GET IT IN...
...ALL THE WAY TO THE CORE ANTENNA.

...
. . .WHAAA?

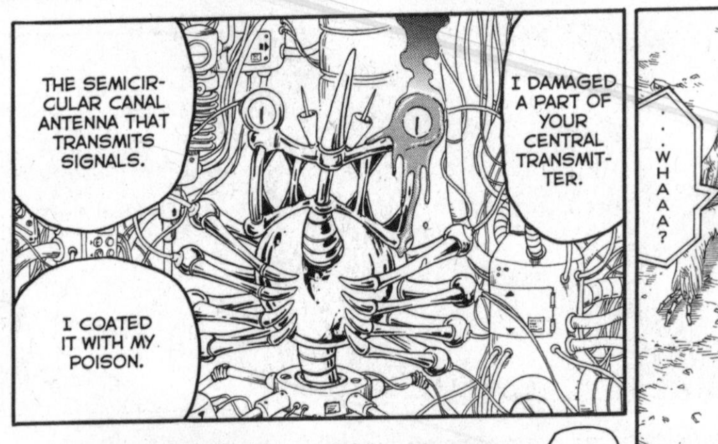
I DAMAGED A PART OF YOUR CENTRAL TRANSMIT-TER.
THE SEMICIR-CULAR CANAL ANTENNA THAT TRANSMITS SIGNALS.
I COATED IT WITH MY POISON.

ALLOW ME TO EXPLAIN.

YOU COULD SAY YOU JUST GOT...
...POISON JAMMED.
...
WHAT NON-SENSE ...

ZOOP

SWOOM

KA-BAMMM

--?!

WHEN HE PRODUCED THE HYDROGEN SULFIDE IN HIS BODY, HE CREATED TWO OTHER POISONS AT THE SAME TIME.

ONE WAS A CONCENTRATED HYDROCHLORIC ACID HE CONSTRUCTED OUT OF STOMACH ACID. THE OTHER WAS A CONCENTRATED NITRIC ACID HE MADE FROM OXIDIZING HIS BODY'S AMMONIA.

HE ALWAYS PLANNED FOR THE HYDROGEN SULFIDE TO IGNITE.
BUT NOT SO IT COULD CAUSE DAMAGE TO THE GT ROBOT.
INSTEAD, HE WANTED TO USE IT AS COVER WHILE HE FIRED THE TWO OTHER POISONS WHILE HE PROTECTED HIS BODY WITH A POISON SHIELD.
THE HEAT OF THE EXPLOSION VAPORIZED THE CONCENTRATED HYDROCHLORIC ACID AND NITRIC ACID, ALLOWING THEM TO PENETRATE THE GT ROBOT'S BODY AND REACH ITS CORE.
MY CORE DOESN'T HAVE THE SAME DURABILITY AS THE REST OF MY BODY, BUT...
WOBBL
WUBBL
...ITS SURFACE IS COATED WITH A HIGHLY CONDUCTIVE METAL.
IS THAT SO?
BECAUSE YOU LOOK AWFULLY UN- STEADY.
SAME GOES FOR YOU.
BOTH ACIDS TRANSITIONED FROM GAS BACK TO LIQUID AND MIXED INSIDE YOUR CORE, THE RATIO OF HYDROCHLORIC ACID TO NITRIC ACID BEING 3:1.
RIGHT ABOUT NOW, THAT LIQUID COMPOUND IS EATING AWAY AT YOUR INNARDS, SO TO SPEAK.

IT'S CALLED *AQUA REGIA*!!

THE MOST CORROSIVE LIQUID KNOWN TO MAN!!

SWOOO

KA—BAMMM

I GUESS THIS BODY IS JUST TOO LARGE TO BE AIRTIGHT.
HOW IRONIC THAT MY GREATEST ASSET BECAME MY DOWNFALL.
SORRY, BUT...
THE FAULT LIES WITH *YOU,* NOT YOUR ROBOT.
ALL IT WOULD HAVE TAKEN TO ASSURE YOUR VICTORY WAS FOR YOU TO KILL ME STRAIGHT OUT, INSTEAD OF IGNITING THE GAS.
YOUR THEAT-RICS PRO-LONGED MY LIFE, AND ASSURED YOUR DEFEAT.
GRRR ...
YOU RIGHTEOUS TWERP!
SKFF
EITHER WAY...
OUR MATCH HAS ENDED.
TELL YOUR HIGHER-UPS...
...THAT COCO ...

THUMP

BOOF

DAMN... I'M OUT...
I USED TOO MUCH... POISON ...

I HAVE TO DRINK SOMETHING ...AND EAT...
BUT TORIKO AND THE OTHERS NEED ME RIGHT NOW...

!

WOOO

TORIKO

GOURMET CHECKLIST

Vol. 030

BATTALION YETI

(MAMMAL)

CAPTURE LEVEL: 2

HABITAT: BATTALION REGION

LENGTH: 2 METERS

HEIGHT: --

WEIGHT: 120 KG

PRICE: 20,000 YEN PER EYEBALL

SCALE

THIS HERBIVOROUS MONKEY ONCE INHABITED THE BATTALION REGION. THE SPECIES WENT EXTINCT DUE TO INFREQUENT BREEDING, BUT THANKS TO CLONING TECHNOLOGY AT THE IGO GOURMET LAB, THE BATTALION YETI HAS A NEW LEASE ON LIFE! YETI EYES ARE IMBUED WITH HIGH AMOUNTS OF DHA AND EPA (ELEMENTS THAT ACTIVATE BRAIN CELLS). EXPERIMENTS ARE UNDERWAY TO MATE THEM WITH ANIMALS THAT HAVE HIGHER REPRODUCTIVE RATES, IN HOPES OF STABILIZING THE POPULATION.

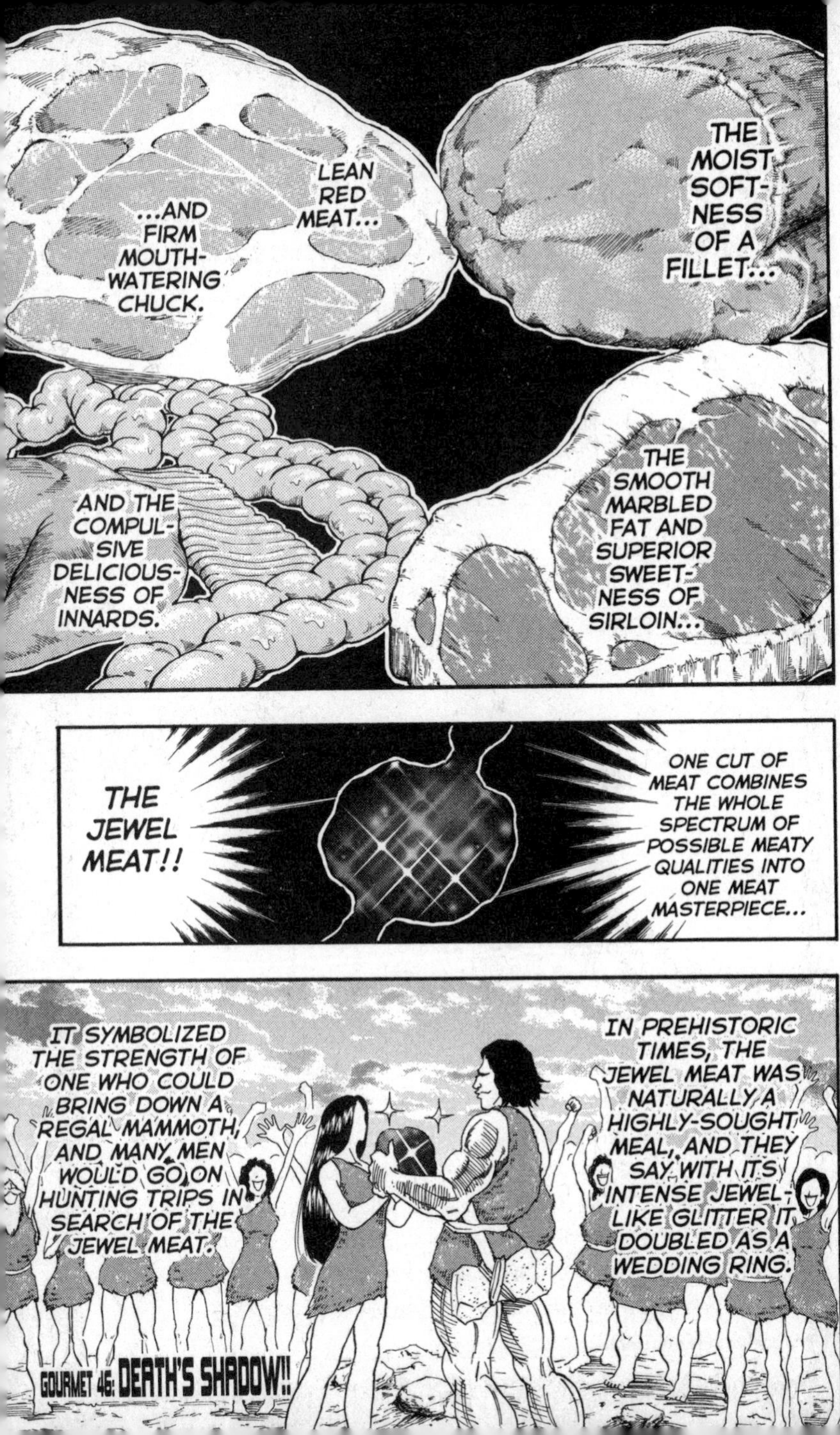

THE MOIST SOFTNESS OF A FILLET...

LEAN RED MEAT...

...AND FIRM MOUTH-WATERING CHUCK.

THE SMOOTH MARBLED FAT AND SUPERIOR SWEETNESS OF SIRLOIN...

AND THE COMPULSIVE DELICIOUSNESS OF INNARDS.

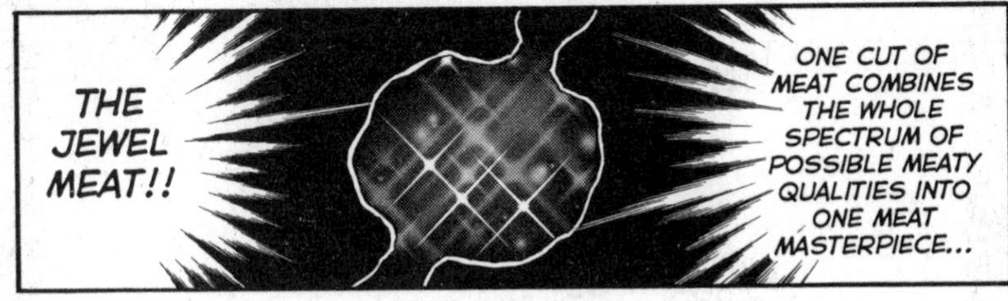

GOURMET 46: DEATH'S SHADOW!!

[WINGS]
AT ONE POINT, THE MAMMOTH MUST HAVE BEEN AN AERIAL CREATURE. THE NON-FUNCTIONAL WINGS ARE SUCCULENT AND TASTE LIKE CHICKEN.
REGAL MAMMOTH (MAMMAL)
CALLED A "FOOD GEM" SINCE ANTIQUITY, THIS GIANT MAMMOTH GROWS LIKE NOBODY'S BUSINESS. JUST A FEW WEEKS AFTER BIRTH, THEY ARE ALREADY 50 METERS IN LENGTH (AND THEY ARE TYPICALLY BORN AROUND 10 METERS LONG). THEY DON'T REPRODUCE OFTEN, BUT THEY HAVE LONG LIFE SPANS, SOMETIMES OVER 500 YEARS OF AGE, DURING WHICH THEY NEVER STOP GROWING. THE MAMMOTH THAT TORIKO AND COMPANY CURRENTLY ARE IN IS 500 YEARS OLD AND OVER 1500 METERS LONG.
[JEWEL MEAT]
ITS LOCATION VARIES FROM ANIMAL TO ANIMAL, MAKING IT HARD TO FIND. RETAIL PRICE: 100 G / 50,000,000 YEN
GOURMET 46: DEATH'S SHADOW!!

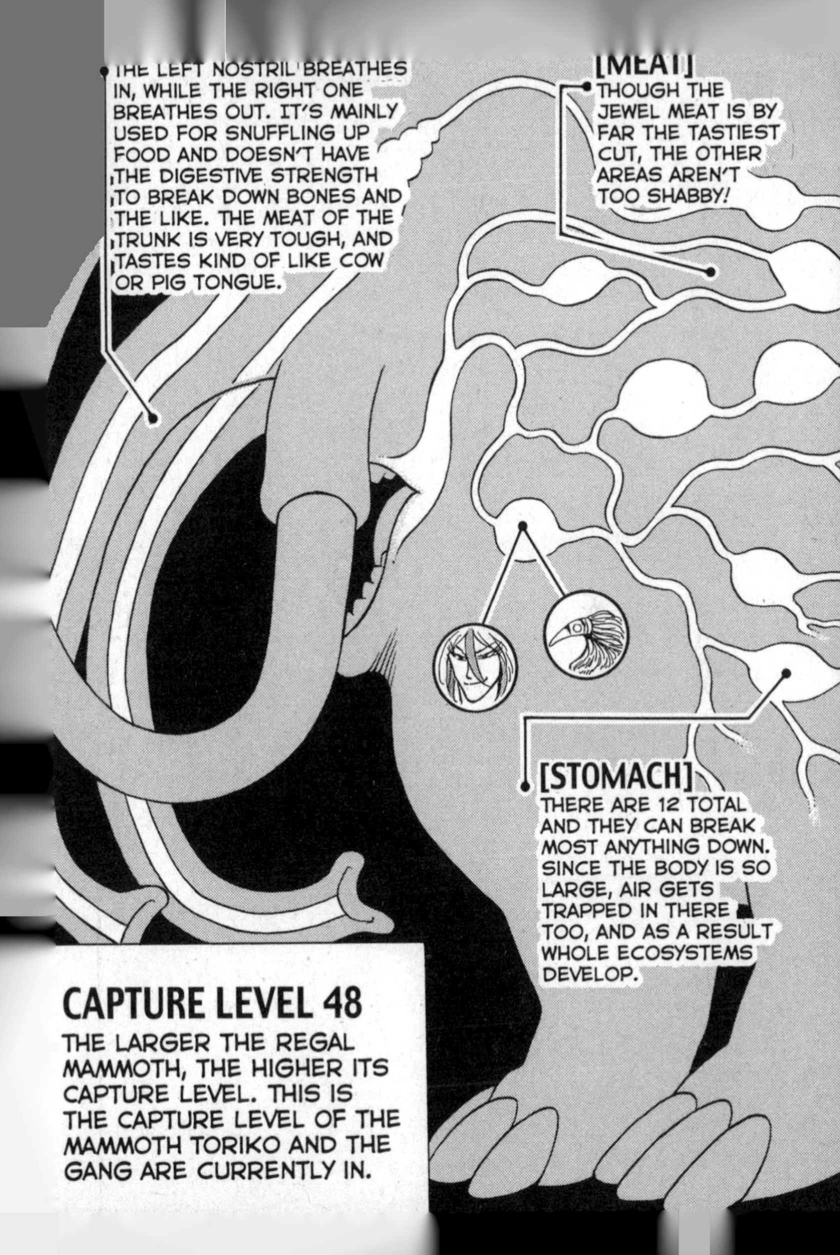

THE LEFT NOSTRIL BREATHES IN, WHILE THE RIGHT ONE BREATHES OUT. IT'S MAINLY USED FOR SNUFFLING UP FOOD AND DOESN'T HAVE THE DIGESTIVE STRENGTH TO BREAK DOWN BONES AND THE LIKE. THE MEAT OF THE TRUNK IS VERY TOUGH, AND TASTES KIND OF LIKE COW OR PIG TONGUE.
[MEAT]
THOUGH THE JEWEL MEAT IS BY FAR THE TASTIEST CUT, THE OTHER AREAS AREN'T TOO SHABBY!
[STOMACH]
THERE ARE 12 TOTAL AND THEY CAN BREAK MOST ANYTHING DOWN. SINCE THE BODY IS SO LARGE, AIR GETS TRAPPED IN THERE TOO, AND AS A RESULT WHOLE ECOSYSTEMS DEVELOP.
CAPTURE LEVEL 48
THE LARGER THE REGAL MAMMOTH, THE HIGHER ITS CAPTURE LEVEL. THIS IS THE CAPTURE LEVEL OF THE MAMMOTH TORIKO AND THE GANG ARE CURRENTLY IN.

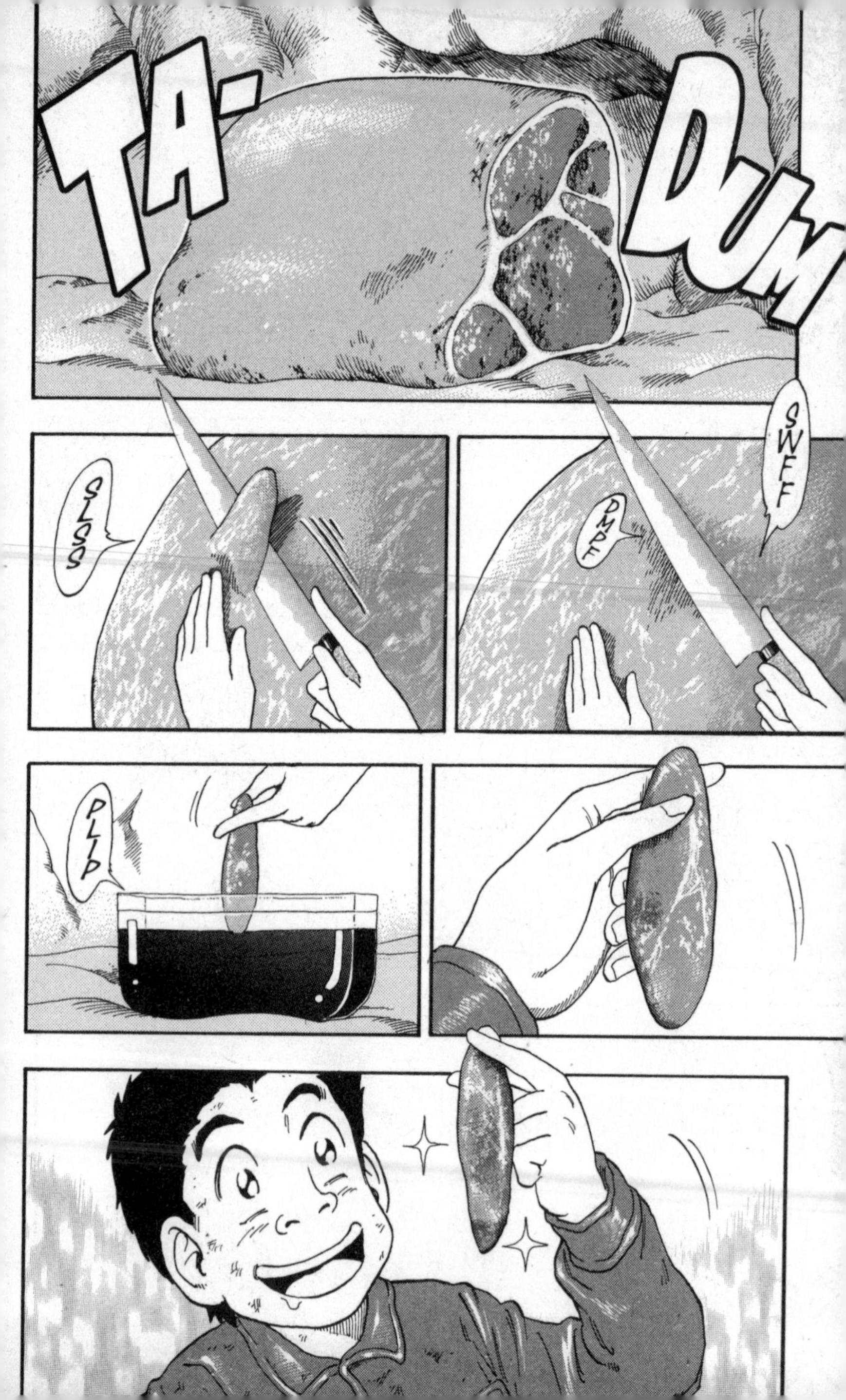
TA-
DUM
SWFF
DMPF
SLSSS
PLIP

AAH

SLUP

NYUM
NYUM
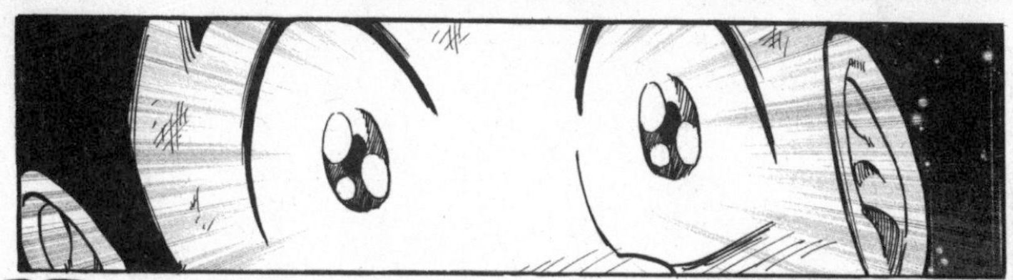

DEEEELISH!
THERE'S JUST ENOUGH FAT TO MAKE IT TENDER AND JUICY! AND THE TASTE'S OUT OF THIS WORLD!
JUDGING BY OUR LOCATION, I'D SAY IT'S RIB ROAST. EVEN UNCOOKED, IT'S AMAZING!

HAVE SOME, RIN.
WE'VE EVEN GOT SOY SAUCE HOPPER SAUCE FOR IT!
COOL! REGAL MAMMOTH ISN'T A DISH I'VE EVER HAD.
I'M SO EXCIT-ED!

TORIKO, WOULD YOU LIKE ANY?
GUYS ...

THE BELLY OF THE BEAST IS NO PLACE TO GET SAUCER-EYED OVER TASTY TREATS. DON'T YOU SEE?
KLP
KLP
THE MAMMOTH'S STOMACH IS ROILING WITH AGITATED CRITTERS.
SNAIL SNAKE
(MOLLUSK)
CAPTURE LEVEL 4
CREATED BY YOSHIKI KOMURO FROM IBARAGI!
ARE WE MAKING THEM MAD BY BEING HERE?
I DON'T THINK SO... AT LEAST, THEY WEREN'T THIS ON EDGE WHEN WE ARRIVED.
SOME-THING'S CHANGED IN THE AIR.
THE AIR'S THICK WITH THE SCENT OF ACID--STOMACH ACID.
THAT CAN ONLY MEAN THE MAMMOTH'S STRESSED OUT FROM SOMETHING. ALMOST AS THOUGH...

...IT'S TRYING TO STAVE OFF SOME KIND OF VIRUS ...
BRRMM
!
...THAT'S INFIL-TRATED ITS BODY!!
WHOOOSH

OH NO! THE MAMMOTH ...
WOOOO
...IS TRYING TO EXPEL ALL FOREIGN ENTITIES FROM ITS BODY!!
THE HOLD OF COCO'S POISON IS PROBABLY WEAKEN-ING.
HURRY, KOMATSU!! RIN!!
UH... AH...
COMING!
HURRY UP, KOMATSU! THIS WAY!
Y-YOU GOT IT!!
WHOOOOOSH
WAH!

...

USUALLY, YOU CAN'T PULL TORIKO AWAY FROM FOOD WITH A CRANE...BUT HE DIDN'T EVEN LOOK TWICE AT THE RIB ROAST...
HE DIDN'T EVEN PESTER ME FOR THE SIRLOIN SHROOMS I HAD ON ME.
COULD HE BE SAVING HIS APPE-TITE FOR THE JEWEL MEAT?
OR...

DA-ZOOM

...COULD IT BE OUR SITUA-TION'S SO BAD...
...THAT HE CAN'T EVEN THINK ABOUT FOOD?

YOU GOTTA BE KID-DING ME.
I DON'T WANT TO BELIEVE IT, BUT...
...THERE'S A POWERFUL OMINOUS AURA CLOGGING UP THE AIR IN HERE.

I HOPE I'M WRONG, BUT...
DID HE MAKE IT IN HERE ?!
IF SO, THEN WE BETTER HOPE WE DON'T RUN INTO HIM!!

WE'VE GOTTA BEAT THAT JERK TO THE PRIZE...
WE HAVE TO FIND THE JEWEL MEAT FIRST!
WOOOOO
SKFF
HYAH HA HA!
COME BACK, YOU COWARD!!
RUNNING AWAY IS DISGUST-ING!!

DWAAP
GWEEE
I'M NOT RUN-NING AWAY!
PYEW PYEW PYEW PYEW PYEW PYEW PYEW PYEW PYEW
HA!
HOW MANY TIMES DO I HAVE TO SAY...
FWOOF
HAIR LEASH!
...YOU'VE GOT NOTHING ON ME.

TLAT
VNEEE
RRN
BA-
BA-
BA-
BO
OM

TYUUM
TYUUM
TYUUM
WOOP
HNGH!
VWEEE
BLA
MM
HYAAAH!!

RRRAH!!!
SPATULA!!!
THOOOOOM
GUH!

WOO-O
WHAT'S THE MATTER?

YOU COULD FIRE A MILLION OF THOSE THINGS MY WAY, AND YOU'D NEVER HIT ME.
SO TOSS THE SPITBALL ACT AND ACTUALLY FIGHT.

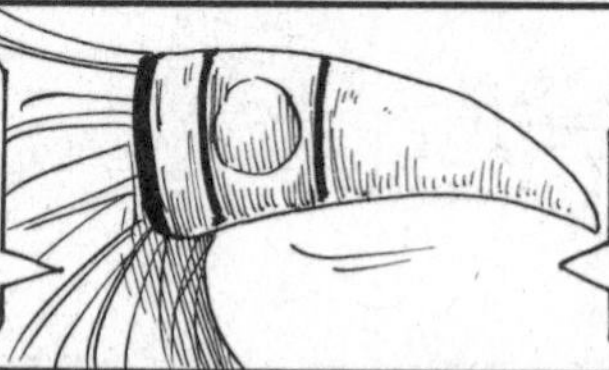
BUT THEN YOU'LL RELEASE THAT UGLY BEAST AGAIN.
IT'S TOO MUCH HASSLE. I'M GOING TO STAY WELL CLEAR OF YOUR RANGE, THANK YOU VERY MUCH.

AND I DON'T NEED TO REMIND YOU THAT YOU CAN'T KEEP UP THAT DODGING ACT FOREVER, DO I?
WAITING AND WATCHING WILL BE QUITE BENEFICIAL TO ME, I THINK... HEE HEE HEE.
DAMN IT...

OUTSIDE, TEN MINUTES PRIOR...
WOOOO

SWIVL
HYUP
...
DZ
OOM
BISH
BISH
BISH
BISH
PLOK

BAOOH
JOLT
WOOOOO
...
AGH...
THAT... THAT ROBOT'S GOING TO KILL SOMEBODY...
SOME-BODY'S... GOING TO DIE...
NO...

TORIKO

GOURMET CHECKLIST

Vol. 031

MUSCLE CRAB

(MAMMAL-CRUSTACEAN HYBRID)

CAPTURE LEVEL: 3

HABITAT: IGO GOURMET LAB

LENGTH: 5 METERS

HEIGHT: 2.5 METERS

WEIGHT: 2 TONS

PRICE: 1 KG / 300,000 YEN

SCALE

THIS CROSS BETWEEN A MUSCLE BISON AND RAZOR CRAB WAS BIOENGINEERED BY THE IGO. THE POWER OF ITS MUSCLES IS ONLY MATCHED BY THE SHARPNESS OF ITS PINCHERS. ALWAYS A FAN FAVORITE IN THE GOURMET COLISEUM!

GOURMET 47: HAIR BATTLE!!

SQUIRM
SQUIRM
WRIGGLE
BLINK
WRIGGLE
SQUIRM
SQUIRM
BLINK

WHAT THE?! THAT'S THE GROSSEST, MOST DISGUSTING-- EWWW!!
!!

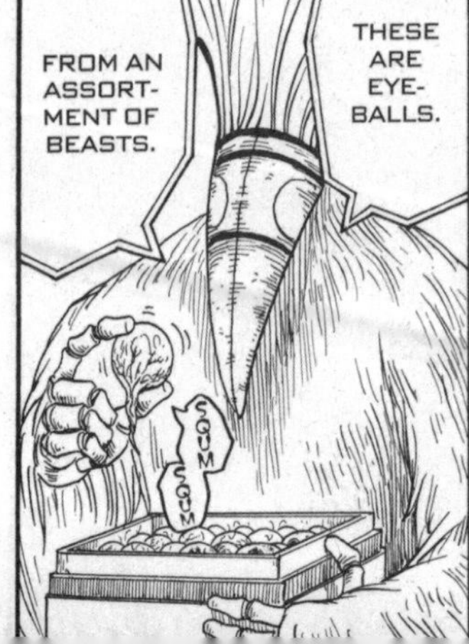

COLLECTING EYEBALLS IS MY HOBBY.
IT'S SO NICE WHEN YOU CAN COLLECT ONES FROM CREATURES YOU REALLY LIKE. ♡
YOU'RE MESSED UP!
DID YOU KNOW THAT THE EYES OF SOME CREATURES CONTINUE TO FUNCTION EVEN AFTER THE BODY IS DEAD?
LIKE HEARTS THAT KEEP BEAT-ING AFTER THE BRAIN HAS DIED.
SQUICKLE
BLINK
THOSE ARE THE KINDS I COLLECT.
LOOK.
WINK!
BLINK ♡
HOW TENDERLY THIS EYE GAZES UPON ME.
MISCHIE-VOUS LITTLE SO-AND-SO...
NASTY!!
I'LL HAVE TO TAKE HIS EYES WHEN I GET THE CHANCE
HIS
AWW...THIS EYEBALL'S STOPPED MOVING. BYE-BYE.
POINK
THIS BASTARD...
I ALMOST FORGOT. EVER SINCE I GOT INSIDE THE MAMMOTH...
...THIS LITTLE FELLA'S GOTTEN AWFULLY FOND OF ME TOO.
SQUEEEM

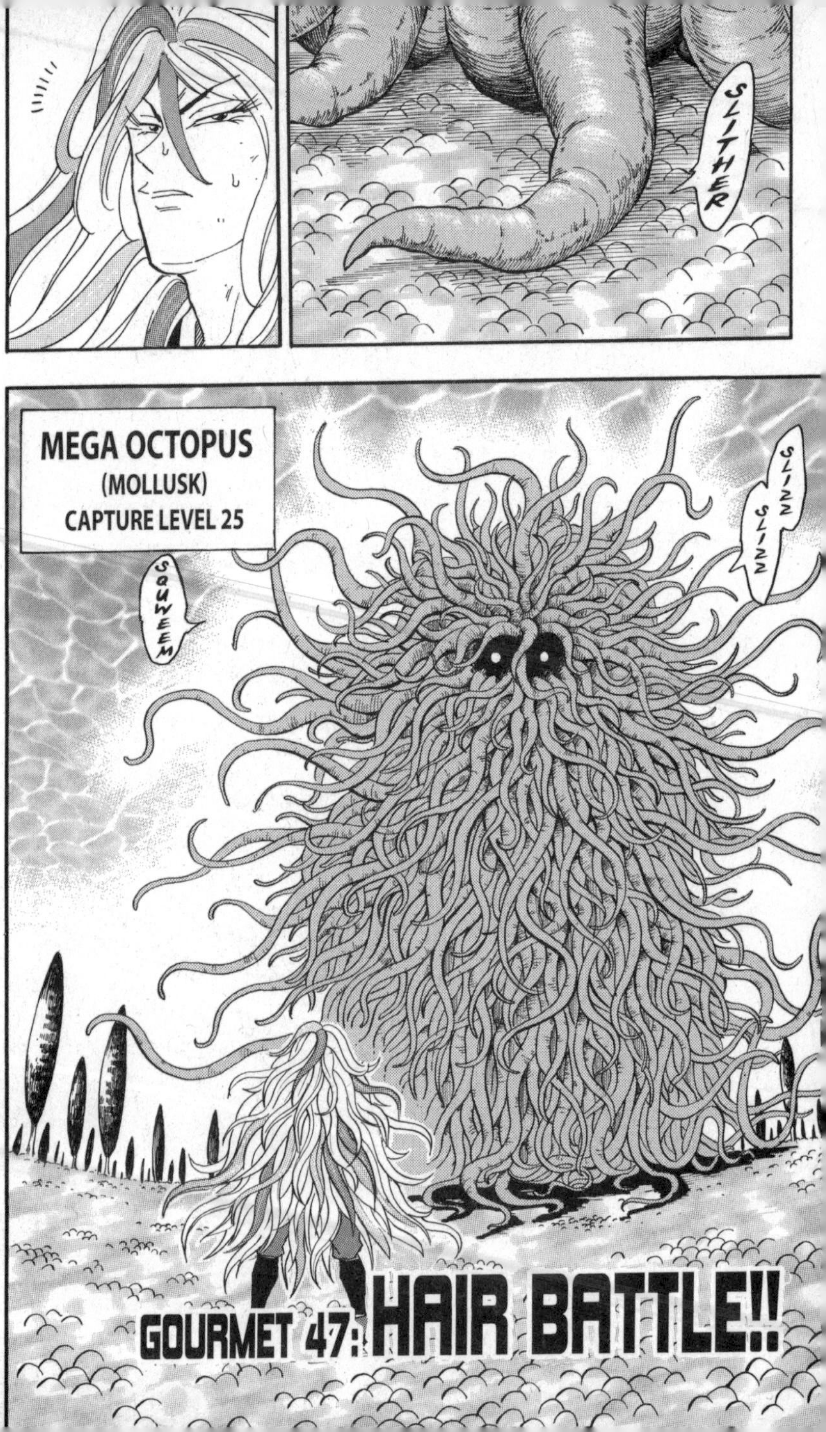

MEGA OCTOPUS
(MOLLUSK)
CAPTURE LEVEL 25

SLIZZ SLIZZ

SQUWEEM

GOURMET 47: HAIR BATTLE!!

EYYWWW!!

WHAT ADORABLE LITTLE EYES IT HAS, DOESN'T IT?

BETTER NOT FORGET TO PLUCK THEM OUT LATER!

BUT FIRST...

MGYAA

WHOOSH

!

WHOA!!

SPATULA!!!
SLAP SLAP SLAP SLAP SLAP SLAP SLAP SLAP
FWIP
WHIZZ

HYAAH! GET ALONG, LITTLE DOGGIE!!
SHAK
MGYAAA
GETTING TOO CLOSE IS A NO-NO.
PUT YOUR BACK INTO IT!!
BUT !!
MIND YOU KEEP YOUR DIS-TANCE.
WHOOSH
!
EVERY STRAND OF HAIR ON HIS HEAD...
...HOLDS A SENSOR HE CAN CONTROL AT WILL.
THOOOM
WHAT CONCEN-TRATION IT MUST TAKE TO ORCHES-TRATE THEM!
HE CAN'T KEEP BLOCKING INDEFI-NITELY.
HE'LL GET POOPED OUT SOONER OR LATER.

QUIT GETTIN IN THE WAY!!
HAIR LOCK!!
SNAAAP
!
SQUIP
SQUIP SQUIP
WHOOSH
WHOA!

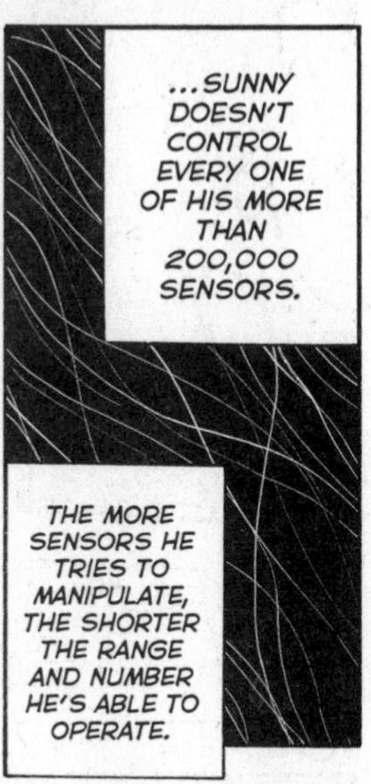

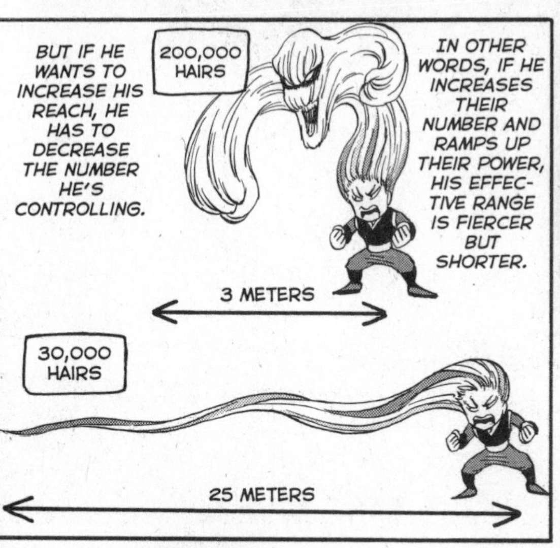

AND SINCE EACH SENSOR HAS NERVES RUNNING THROUGH IT...

AS HE TIRES, HE BEGINS ROTATING OUT HAIRS.

THE LONGEST HE CAN KEEP USING HIS SENSORS IS AROUND AN HOUR.

SUNNY KNOWS THIS GOING INTO ANY BATTLE.

UN-
FORTU-
NATELY
...
TWAAAAK
...HIS
CURRENT
BATTLE
CALLED
FOR MORE
THAN
50,000
SENSORS!
WHEN
FORCED TO
EXCEED
THIS
THRESHOLD
...
...SUNNY'S
LIMITED AS
TO HOW
LONG HE CAN
USE HIS
SENSORS.
IT'S A SMALL BUT
EXPLOITABLE WEAK
SPOT IN HIS
TYPICALLY
INVINCIBLE
"DINING KITCHEN."

HAH...
POOF
I QUIT.
IT'S NOT WORTH IT.
!!
SUNNY RETRACTED HIS SENSORS.
IT WASN'T IN HIS NATURE TO LET A FIGHT BECOME A BATTLE OF WITS.
NOR WAS HE THE TYPE TO FIGHT TOOTH AND NAIL TO AVOID DEFEAT.
NO, WHAT SUNNY LIKED...
THERE, I'M DEFENSELESS. SO COME AND GET ME, OCTOPUSSY.
...WAS A FLAWLESS FIGHT WITH A TIDY RESOLUTION.

AAAAH!
RAAAAAWR!!
DUM
DUM
DUM
KERACK
AAAARGH!!
ONLY A PERFECT RESOLUTION...
BOOF
HYAAAH!
...WAS EXQUISITE ENOUGH TO SATISFY SUNNY.

TH
UP
HYEEE!
BAMM
SPOOOO
HYAH HYAH HYAH! OOOH, JUST WHAT THE DOCTOR ORDERED!!
AS SOON AS I SAW THAT PRETTY-BOY FACE OF YOURS...
...I'VE WANTED TO SMASH IT IN!!
ASH

RRR...
RRR
...HUH?
SAME HERE.
GO, HAIR LOCK...
THIS WHOLE TIME I'VE WANTED TO SMASH IN YOUR UGLY MUG!
ZANG
HEY, OCTOPUS, WHY AREN'T YOU ATTACKING HIM?! GET TO IT!! MUSH!
LAUGHABLE.
LOOK AT ITS EYES. THERE ISN'T A LICK OF CONCERN FOR YOU IN THEM.
THEY'RE NOTHING BUT AFRAID.
JUST LIKE...
...WHAT I SEE IN YOUR EYES RIGHT NOW.
LOOOOM
UH-OH.
NOT AGAIN...

VOO, OOO!
I'VE TAKEN YOUR PUNCHES.
NOW IT'S YOUR TURN TO TAKE MINE.
TCH...
RRRRI...
NO THANKS!
VWEEEE
RRRRR...
20,000 STRAND
...

...HAIR PUNCH!!!
THOOM

OP

YOU'RE ONE TOUGH BASTARD.
I'M ACTUALLY SHOCKED YOU DIDN'T SHATTER FROM MY 20,000 STRAND HAIR PUNCH.

S-S-SH-H-H
YOU... STUPID ...
PAY-BACK ...

...WILL BE HELL...
...

WHO SAID ANYTHING ABOUT LETTING YOU ATTACK?! HA! AS IF!
THE ONLY OPENING YOU'LL BE GETTING IS IN YOUR SKULL!
...!!
JUST KIDDING. HA HA HA!
DID I DO A GOOD IMPERSON-ATION OF YOU?
...!!
WHY, YOU ...
BAH
OH, YEAH. I FORGOT TO MENTION ...
WHEN I USED MY HAIR PUNCH ON YOU, I SNUCK SOME SENSORS INSIDE YOU.
THEY'VE ENTANGLED YOUR CORE.
JUST THINK... SOME 10,000 OR SO ODD SENSORS GRIPPING YOU TIGHTER AND TIGHTER WITH EVERY MOVE YOU MAKE.
SO HERE'S A WORD OF ADVICE...
I BETTER PUT SOME DISTANCE BETWEEN US.
HOP
I CAN'T BE SURE I'LL BE LUCKY ENOUGH TO SURVIVE ANOTHER PUNCH LIKE THAT.

YOU BETTER NOT STRAY TOO FAR FROM ME.
OR YOU'LL BE SORRY.
GOTTA GET OUT OF RANGE!
FAR, FAR AWAY!
SKRRRRRCH
AP
OOF!
BZZT BZZT
KRIK
KRAKL
...?!
...AGH!
ZZRT
JERK
SEE, TOLD YOU SO.
TOO BAD IT'S SUCH AN UGLY VICTORY, BUT...
...THERE'S SOME VINDICATION IN SEEING YOU WRITHE LIKE THE SPINELESS COWARD YOU ARE.

TORIKO

GOURMET CHECKLIST

Vol. 032

ELEPHANTSAURUS

(REPTILE)

CAPTURE LEVEL: 17

HABITAT: NORTHERN CONTINENT

LENGTH: 15 METERS

HEIGHT: 6.5 METERS

WEIGHT: 10 TONS

PRICE: 1 KG / 250,000 YEN (MEAT), 300,000,000 YEN PER TUSK

SCALE

THIS ELEPHANTINE REPTILE HAS A HEAD WHERE ITS TRUNK SHOULD BE! IT'S A SLOW MOVER, BUT CONSIDERING ITS GREATEST ADVANTAGE IS MASQUERADING AS A PLANT-EATER, IT DOESN'T NEED TO MOVE FAST TO CATCH PREY. ELEPHANT-SAURUS TUSKS ARE SAID TO BRING LUCK.

HOW...

...DID YOU REACH MY CORE ...?!

HOW, YOU ASK? MY SENSORS ARE .1 MICRONS THICK.

THEY CAN PASS THROUGH GAPS THE SIZE OF PORES EASILY.

GOURMET 48: THE WORST ENCOUNTER!!

UNGH ...
THWAMMM
...!!
GOURMET 48: THE WORST ENCOUNTER!!
THUD
HANH!
HANH!

AAAAW, I'M BUSHED !!
DAMN IT ALL!
SPLAT
I CAN'T BELIEVE I LET SOMEONE STRIKE ME IN THE FACE AGAIN!
ARGH ...
HE REALLY DID A NUMBER ON ME.
WHEN I GET MY HANDS ON THAT OPERATOR, I'LL...
BRRRMM...
HMM?
WHOOSH
WHOA, WHAT THE ?!
WAAAAAH!!

SNOOF
SNOOF
BFFUUU
...!
DWAAH!!
WHOOOSH
!
SUNNY!!!

KISS, GET HIM!!

FWAP

WHOOSH

SWUP

APH!

I JUST FELL DOWN INCREDIBLY HARD!

I'M SURE YOU DID...

WELL, IT WOULD TAKE A LOT TO BRING HIM DOWN.

SO THAT SHADOW OF DEATH WASN'T SUNNY'S...

THE STRONG ELECTRO-MAGNETIC WAVE I SENSED INITIALLY FROM THE MAMMOTH...

SUNNY PROBABLY TOOK CARE OF HIM.

I TROUNCED THAT GUY! LIKE TAKING CANDY FROM A BABY!

BUT NOW...

... THERE'S A NEW ROBOT IN THERE!

AND NOW I KNOW THAT SHADOW OF DEATH IS FOR SOMEBODY IN TORIKO'S GROUP!

WE HAVE TO HURRY, SUNNY!

TORIKO AND THE OTHERS ARE IN DANGER!

HUH?

UUH ...

WURBL

WHAT'S THE DEAL, COCO? GET COLD FEET?

IT'S NOT LIKE YOU TO WEENY OUT.

FWUMP
AND I'M SORRY, BUT I DESERVE A BREAK.
PLUS THERE'S ABSOLUTELY NO WAY I'M GOING BACK INSIDE THAT MAMMOTH.
PLOP

BUT SUNNY ...
THE ROBOT LEFT INSIDE THE MAMMOTH ...
GULP
YOU ALWAYS WERE A WORRY-WART, COCO.

YOU AND I HAVE ALREADY PLAYED OUR PARTS.
CHUG
CHUG
THE MOMENT WE PUT TORIKO IN CHARGE OF GETTING THE JEWEL MEAT, WE DECIDED THAT.

BESIDES, DON'T YOU THINK IT'S INSULTING TO TORIKO IF WE WENT IN TO HELP?
SOME-BODY'S GOING TO *DIE*.
SO?
...
ARE YOU SAYING THE ALMIGHTY *TORIKO* IS GOING TO FAIL?
...

BELIEVE IN HIM.
FAITH IN YOUR FRIENDS IS A BEAUTIFUL THING.

D-DASH
VEER TO THE RIGHT!
WHOOSH
WHOA!
WOW!

A-AMAZING!

THIS WHOLE PLACE IS *GLEAMING*!!

WHERE ARE WE NOW, TORIKO?

THE FLESH HERE IS REFLECTING THE GLEAM FROM THE JEWEL MEAT.

YEP.

THE JEWEL MEAT'S NOT FAR, KOMATSU!

OOOOH! OF COURSE JEWEL MEAT WOULD SHINE LIKE A JEWEL! THAT TOTALLY EXPLAINS WHY IT'S SO BRIGHT INSIDE THE MAMMOTH.

YUMMM! IT SMELLS SO GOOD IN HERE! ♡

!
HUH?
RUN, KOMATSU!!!

GET OUTTA HERE!!!

GYAAAAAAH!!!
TORIKO?!!
SKRITCH SKRITCH
HE DIDN'T EVEN FLINCH...
...AT MY INTIMIDATION!!
FIVE-FOLD...

SWUP
KRAK
!!
THWUMP

OOOOOO
WHIP
BSSH
!
WELL, WELL.
HE GRAZED ME.

WAAAAAH!!!
YOINK
TORIKO!!!!
SWEFF
SWIVL
K-KLIK
FRA-
GRANCE
BAZOO-
KA!!
SWIP
BSH
OOM

BA
DUM
!!!
SPLURCH

TORIKO

GOURMET CHECKLIST

Vol. 033

GROWLRUS

(MAMMAL)

CAPTURE LEVEL: 13

HABITAT: TUNDRA

LENGTH: 7.8 METERS

HEIGHT: 4.1 METERS

WEIGHT: 6.5 TONS

PRICE: 83,000 YEN EACH

SCALE

THIS ISN'T YOUR MOTHER'S WALRUS! THE GROWLRUS, AKA THE AMPHIBIOUS DEVIL, BOASTS EXCEPTIONAL BLUBBER THAT ALLOWS IT TO SURVIVE BOTH SUB-ZERO CLIMATES AND SUBSTANTIALLY WEAKENS THE IMPACT OF ENEMY ATTACKS. IT'S A FAVORITE OF NEWBIES TO THE GOURMET COLISEUM SCENE, AND PEOPLE OFTEN ADVISE THAT "IF YOU DON'T KNOW WHO TO GO WITH, BET ON THE GROWLRUS."

GOURMET 49: SIGN OF EVOLUTION!!

SHLORP
CHOMP
HUH ?!

WHA...
SLURP
SMACK
WHAT THE ...?!

WHO IS HE ...?

THAT'S ME!
HE'S EATING ME?!

YOUR TIME LIMIT ...
...IS FIVE MINUTES.

DEVOUR SOME-THING.
YES...
THE MORE WORTHY IT IS OF BEING SAVORED, THE BETTER.
DO THAT...
...AND YOUR CELLS WILL EVOLVE.
TORIKO !!!
RIN !!!
FWOOF
FWOOF
PRIK
...
NN ...

...
FWOOF
FWOOF
TH...
THIS IS...

PSHOOM

THIS IS ENDORPHIN SMOKE!!
TO...
TORI... KO...

AT LEAST... IT'LL...
...TAKE AWAY... THE PAIN...

RIN...
YOU...
RRRR
...PUT ME...
...BEFORE YOURSELF...?

RRRMM
WAAAAAH!!

HAD YOU GUYS STAYED OUT OF MY WAY...
THOMP
!!

HEY.
WHO YOU CALLING DEAD?
!

KLAAANG
THOOOO
MO
HNGH
HNGH

RIN...

...
HNFF...
KOFF
HNFF...
TO... RI...

DON'T SPEAK, RIN.
THE... SCAR ...
...UNDER MY... EYE...

I DID IT...
...TO MYSELF.

I WANTED TO LOOK... LIKE YOU, TORIKO.
HEH HEH...
BUT I MIXED UP...MY RIGHT AND LEFT...
THAT'S WHY...I STOPPED AFTER ONLY ONE ...
RIN ...

T...
TORI... KO...
CAN YOU...
...DO ME...

...A FAVOR...
...PLEASE?

I WILL.

POP

IMPOSSIBLE...

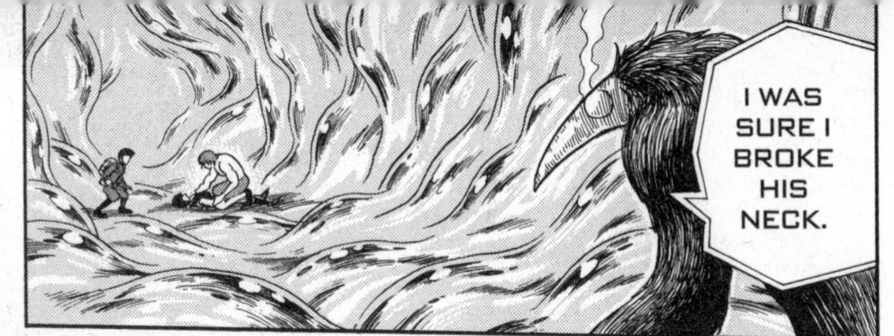
I WAS SURE I BROKE HIS NECK.

THANK...YOU...
TORI...KO...

POP POP
NO WAY...
THIS POWER IS--
WER

TO
C'MERE ...
...GT ROBOT!!
GOURMET 49: SIGN OF EVOLUTION!!

GTRO
RO
BOOOOT!!!
PZOOOM
!
FORK!!!
BAMMM
HMMPH!
SLA
!!

HAKK!
KNIFE !!
SL!
!!
POP POP
FIVE ...
SIX ...
SIX-FOLD ...

SPIKED PUNCH!!!
BAM BAM BADABAM
THWUP
THWUP

BAM
THWUP
THWUP
THWOOP
THWUP

BOOOOOOOM

RIN ACCEPTED...

...THAT SHE MIGHT DIE TODAY.

EVERY LIVING CREATURE IN THE WILD...

...ACCEPTS THAT DANGER.

BUT BEING IN THAT MECHANICAL SUIT, YOU LACK ALL OF THAT WILD INSTINCT.

SO LET ME *SHOW* YOU!!

WHEREVER YOU MAY BE...

I'LL SHOW YOU...

...HOW TERRIFYING DEATH CAN BE.

WAS THAT A COINCIDENCE?

OR HIS CHOICE?

HE'S UNDERGOING AUTOPHAGY.

THAT'S THE FIRST SIGN.

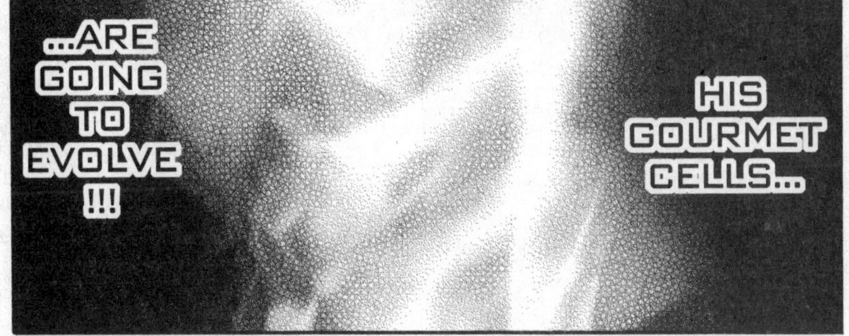

TORIKO

GOURMET CHECKLIST

Vol. 034

GEROLUD

(AVIAN)

CAPTURE LEVEL: 15

HABITAT: MOUNTAINS

LENGTH: 13 METERS

HEIGHT: 8.7 METERS

WEIGHT: 5.6 TONS

PRICE: 1 KG / 120,000 YEN

SCALE

AN AVIAN TERROR SPORTING FIVE HEADS FROM AN OSTRICH BODY CERTAINLY DESERVES ITS NICKNAME OF GRIM REAPER OF THE SKIES. EACH OF THE FIVE HEADS IS COMPLETELY AUTONOMOUS, SO IT IS CAPABLE OF PECKING OUT AN ENEMY'S EYES WITH ONE SHARP BEAK WHILE USING ITS LONG NECK TO WRAP AROUND ANOTHER ENEMY AT THE SAME TIME. WHEN ATTACKED, IT CAN USE ITS WINGS TO ESCAPE INTO THE SKIES, JABBING AND DODGING ALL THE WHILE. IT'S NO WONDER THIS FORMIDABLE WARRIOR IS FAMOUS IN GOURMET COLISEUM CIRCLES.

GOURMET 50: FIVE-MINUTE TIME LIMIT!!

THOUGH BEAUTIFUL TO BEHOLD ...
...IT WASN'T THE VIEW OF THE UNDERWATER GARDEN THAT WAS DIVINE.
IT WAS HOW IT TASTED.

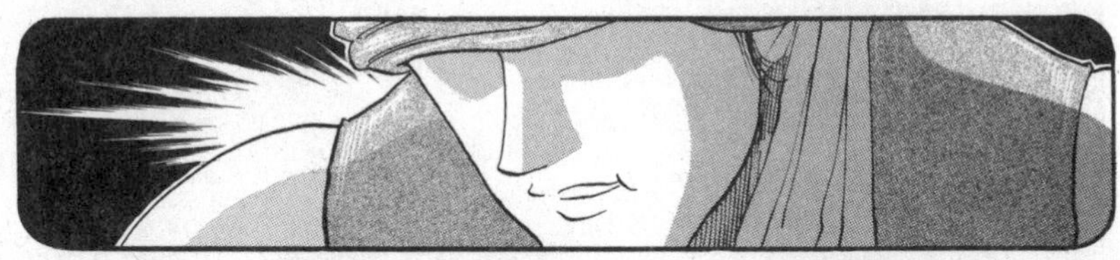

THE FLAVOR OF THE FIRST FISH HE ATE THERE ...
... BROUGHT ACACIA TO TEARS.

THERE WERE NO WORDS TO DE-SCRIBE THE TASTE.
AAAH ...
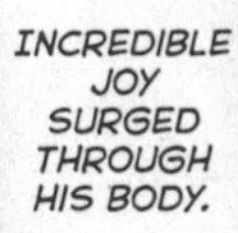
INCREDIBLE JOY SURGED THROUGH HIS BODY.

UNTIL THIS VERY MOMENT ...
...I NEVER TRULY LIVED.
IT WAS IF HE HAD BEEN REBORN.

AND SO HIS DAYS OF RESEARCH BEGAN.

WHAT ARE THESE FLAVOR COMPONENTS?

I'VE NEVER SEEN A SHAPE LIKE THIS BEFORE.

AND ...

SUCH ACTIVE CELLS.

WHERE DO THEY PULL THEIR ENERGY FROM?

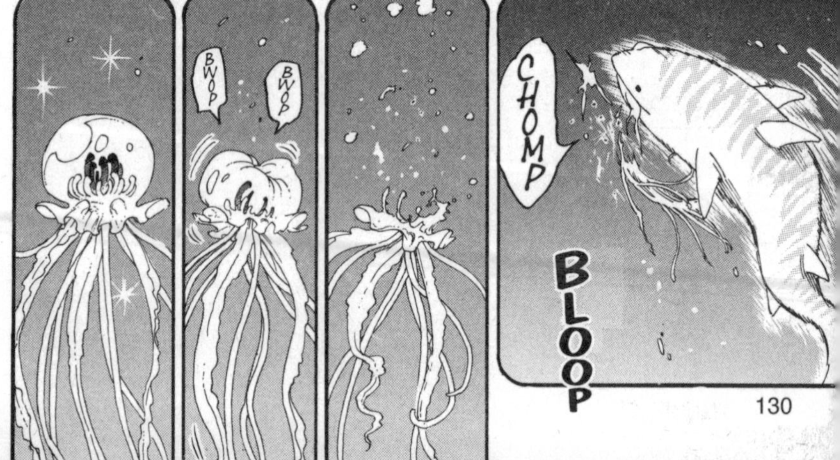

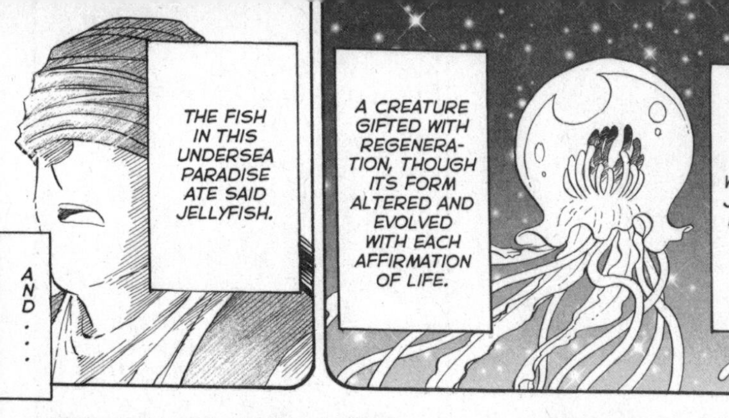
IT WAS A JELLYFISH.
A CREATURE GIFTED WITH REGENERATION, THOUGH ITS FORM ALTERED AND EVOLVED WITH EACH AFFIRMATION OF LIFE.
THE FISH IN THIS UNDERSEA PARADISE ATE SAID JELLYFISH.
AND . . .

...THE FISH WHO ATE THE JELLYFISH...
...ACUTELY INCREASED IN FLAVOR.

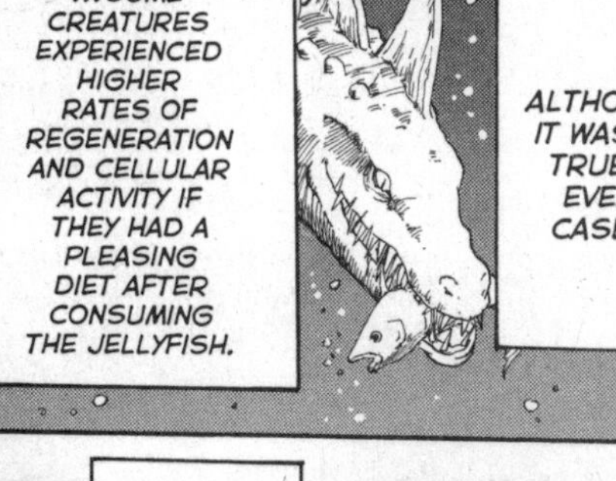
ALTHOUGH IT WASN'T TRUE IN EVERY CASE...
...SOME CREATURES EXPERIENCED HIGHER RATES OF REGENERATION AND CELLULAR ACTIVITY IF THEY HAD A PLEASING DIET AFTER CONSUMING THE JELLYFISH.

AMAZING.
IF I COULD UTILIZE THIS COMPONENT OF THE JELLYFISH, I COULD SELECTIVELY BREED ANY KIND OF INGREDIENT.
AND MOREOVER ...

IT'S LIKE...IT GIVES THEM THE POWER TO EVOLVE.
ACACIA NAMED THE JELLYFISH "GOURMET JELLYFISH" ...
...AND EXTRACTED THE SPECIAL CELLS FROM IT.

HE CALLED THEM GOURMET CELLS.

BRRRRUUMM

YOUR AUTOPHAGY'S BEEN ACTIVATED.
WERE YOU FASTING OR SOMETHING?

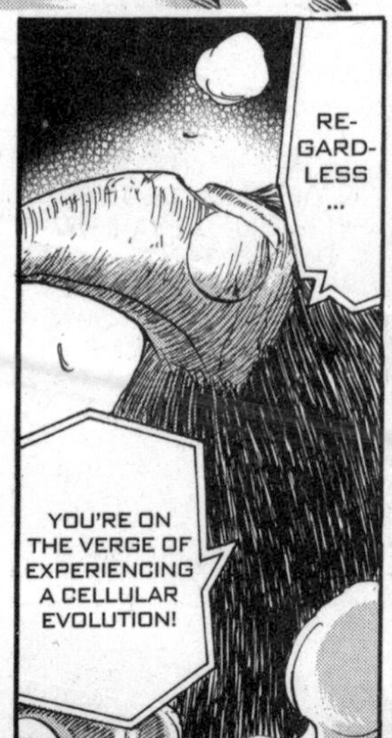
REGARDLESS...
YOU'RE ON THE VERGE OF EXPERIENCING A CELLULAR EVOLUTION!

RR
UMMBL
GOURMET 50: FIVE-MINUTE TIME LIMIT!!
AUTOPHAGY:
THE PROCESS BY WHICH AN ORGANISM THAT IS STARVING FOR NUTRIENTS WILL BREAK DOWN ITS OWN CELL'S PROTEINS INTO AMINO ACIDS TO GIVE IT A BOOST OF ENERGY.
TORIKO GENERALLY BURNS ANYWHERE FROM 100,000 TO 1,000,000 CALORIES IN A DAY.
EVEN SKIPPING A SNACK COULD HAVE SERIOUS CONSE-QUENCES!

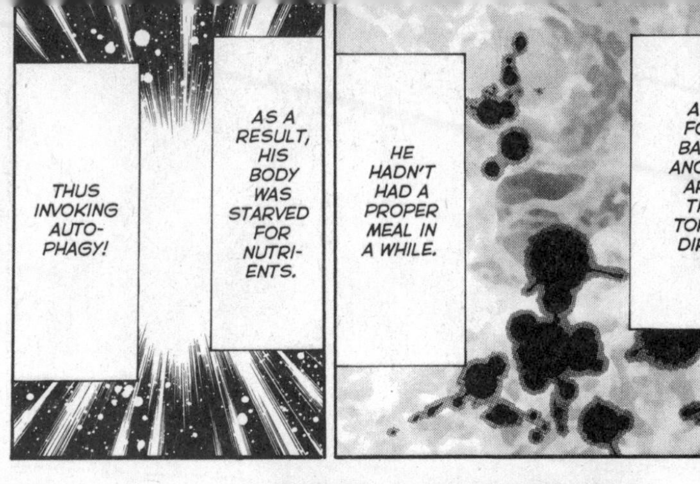

...HE NEEDED AN EVOLU-TION ...

...TO UNLEASH THE FEROCIOUS POWER WITHIN HIM!!

ZOOM

FWIP
FORK !!
HMMPH !
KNIFE !!
KLANG
DWAAP
KTUM
SHUT YOUR BEAK !!
!
RRRAH !!

KATHOOOM
UHHH ...
... RY-AAAAH !!
KATHOOOM
TORIKO!
AMAZ-ING!
...
WOOOO
WHAT TO DO, WHAT TO DO...

SPEED.
POWER.
IN THIS GT ROBOT, I CAN'T UNLEASH EVEN A FRACTION OF MY TRUE POWER.
GOURMET HUNTER TORIKO.
I'M FASCINATED BY YOUR INCREDIBLE POWER.
THIS BODY'S ALREADY CRUMBLING.
BUT THAT POWER OF YOURS...
...
...CAN'T LAST VERY MUCH LONGER.
AUTOPHAGY IS NOTHING MORE THAN A TEMPORARY STOP ON NUTRITIONAL DEPRIVATION.
IF YOU KEEP THAT UP FOR TOO LONG, YOU'LL END UP CONSUMING ALL YOUR CELLS.
INSTEAD OF EVOLUTION, YOU'LL FACE EXTINCTION!
HOW LONG DO YOU HAVE?
AND CAN YOU BEAT ME IN THAT TIME FRAME?

YOUR TIME LIMIT ...

...IS FIVE MIN-UTES.

IT'S USE-LESS!

DUM

BA

SS

SPLI

!!

RI

YAAAH!

B-DOONG

MIXER PUNCH !!

AGH ...

THUNN

!!

UGWAAAH!!

VRRRR

...!
GAH!
VRRR
...
SIX...
SEVEN ... FOLD ...
AGH ...

DAMN IT.
I NEED MORE POWER...

DEVOUR SOMETHING.
YES...
THE MORE WORTHY IT IS OF BEING SAVORED, THE BETTER.

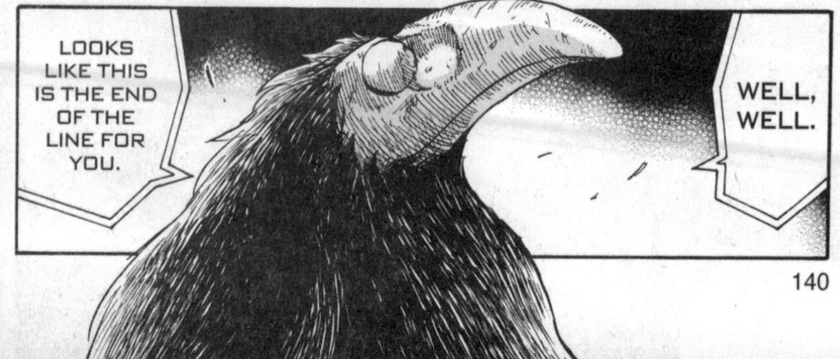
WELL, WELL.
LOOKS LIKE THIS IS THE END OF THE LINE FOR YOU.

FARE-WELL...

... GOURMET HUNTER TORIKO!!

TORIKO!!

VEEEE

WHOOSH

BOOOOOOOM
RR-RR-RRIP
THUM
THWUD

GOURMET CHECKLIST

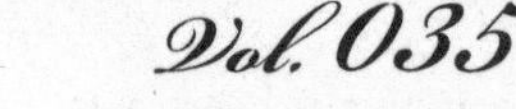

BATTLE WOLF
(MAMMAL)

CAPTURE LEVEL: UNDETERMINED

HABITAT: DETAILS UNKNOWN

LENGTH: 18 METERS

HEIGHT: 8 METERS

WEIGHT: 11 TONS

PRICE: UNKNOWN

SCALE

AN IMMENSELY LARGE AND POWERFUL ANCIENT WOLF. THE IGO GOURMET LAB CLONED A NEW WOLF, BUT LITTLE IS KNOWN REGARDING THEIR HABITS, CAPTURE LEVEL, ETC. THE BATTLE WOLF NAMED TERRY CLOTH WAS BORN FROM THAT CLONED WOLF, AND COULD VERY WELL BE THE LAST BATTLE WOLF IN EXISTENCE. TERRY HAS AN ACUTE SENSE OF DANGER AND HOW TO GET OUT OF IT, WHICH LEADS HIM TO BE WARY AROUND ANYONE BUT TORIKO. HE TRUSTS TORIKO, AND WILL EAT FROM HIS HAND, ROLL OVER AND SHOW HIM HIS BELLY, AND OTHER SUCH ENDEARING BEHAVIORS THAT USUALLY ONLY EXIST BETWEEN PARENT AND CHILD. HOWEVER, HE'S FAR FROM PLAYFUL IN A FIGHT, AND DESPITE HIS TENDER AGE, HE'S KING OF THE TUNDRA.

GOURMET 51: GET READY!!

THE JEWEL MEAT!!
IN THE SPACE OF A SECOND ...
... FROM A BODY THAT SHOULD HAVE BEEN ...
... COM-PLETELY DEHY-DRATED ...
...BE IT SWEAT...
...OR EVEN DROPS OF BLOOD ...

...TORIKO'S MOUTH SUDDEN-LY GUSHED SALIVA.
SPLOOSH
AT THE SAME TIME...
...HIS BROKEN BODY...
...WHICH SHOULD HAVE BEEN PARALYZED ...
...WALKED TOWARD THE JEWEL MEAT...
...LIKE A MOTH DRAWN TO LIGHT.
A...
AMAZING ...
WHAT GOR-GEOUS MEAT.
MARBLED SO EXQUI-SITELY...
...LIKE IT WAS SCULPTED BY A THOSAND MASTERS!

THE JUICE DRIBBLING OFF OF IT...
...GLIMMERS LIKE GOLDEN SAND!

AND SATURATING EVERYTHING...
THIS AROMA...

THIS INTOXICATING AROMA...
...THAT PUTS EVEN THE MOST EXPENSIVE PERFUMES TO SHAME.

A SCENT THAT BYPASSES SUCH ARTIFICIAL FINERIES...
...AND INSTEAD STIMULATES OUR PRIMAL CRAVINGS.

OHH...
...REGAL MAMMOTH...
...THIS IS BEYOND WORDS!

AND SO HUMBLY...

...I GIVE THANKS.

NOW LET'S EAT!

GOURMET 51: GET READY!!

JUST AS PEOPLE SEE THEIR LIVES FLASH BEFORE THEIR EYES IN A CRISIS...

...TORIKO'S EMOTIONS PASSED THROUGH EVERY STATE DURING THAT INTERVAL.

IN OTHER WORDS, DISCOVERY OF THE JEWEL MEAT...
...WAS A LIFE-OR-DEATH EXPERIENCE FOR TORIKO.

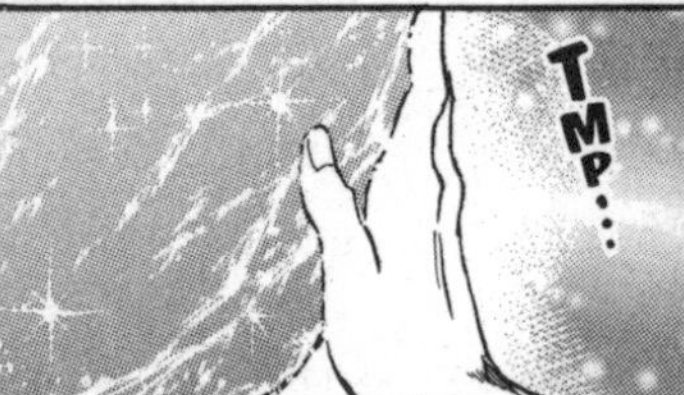
TMP...

IT'S SO SOFT.
IT'S SLIGHTLY WET AND STICKS TO MY SKIN.

KNIFE...
SLSS
BYOING

WOW.
THE JUICES FLYING OFF GLITTER LIKE FIRE-WORKS.

DROOL

GULP

MMPH
MM.
NYUM NYUM
NYUM
NYUM
NYUM NYUM
NYUM NYUM NYUM
NYUM
NYUM
NYUM

GULP

HAAGH...

SO GOOD...

GOOSH

SO, SO GOOD...

RIP
RIP
CHOMP
DELI-CIOUS!
SHLORP
SHLORP
SHLORP
OH, GOD!
THAT FIRST PIECE WAS WET AND SOFT, BUT THIS...
...HAS AN AMAZING TEXTURE!
CHAWM CHAWM
CHAWM CHAWM
NICE AND FIRM, LIKE LIVER!
AND ALL THE JUICE, IT MIGHT FILL MY STOMACH!
IT'S ALMOST TOO MUCH!
SSSSSSS
PING
I CAN'T TAKE MUCH MORE!!
TWANG

LOOKS LIKE YOU...
...WERE THE SMARTEST OF THE BUNCH, LITTLE MAN.
KLAK

HUFF!
HUFF!

EVERYBODY DIES EVENTUALLY.
THERE'S NO NEED TO HURRY YOU ALONG.

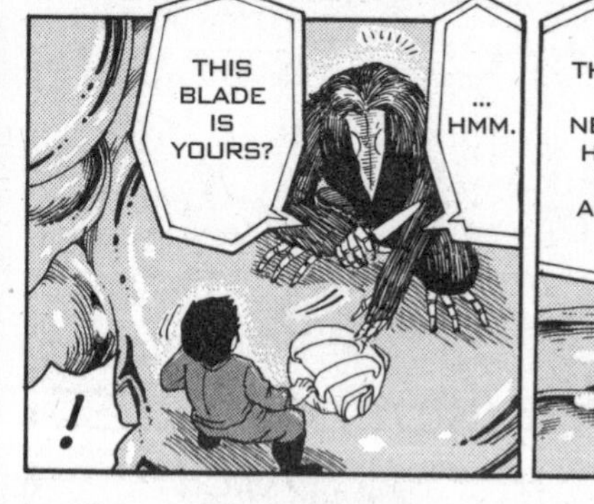
... HMM.
THIS BLADE IS YOURS?
!

IT'S A GOOD KNIFE. YOU CAN LEARN A LOT ABOUT A CHEF'S ABILITY FROM HIS CUTLERY.
THIS KNIFE SAYS... YOU'RE AN ESTEEMED CHEF.

YOU BETTER SHARPEN YOUR SKILLS THOUGH.
IF YOU...
...SOME-DAY ARE TO BE OF USE TO US AT GOUR-MET CORP.

I'LL BE TAKING THIS KNIFE WITH ME.
HEH HEH. IT'LL BE QUITE HANDY.

GRAB
HMM?

THAT...
THAT'S THE ONE THING...
...I CAN'T LET YOU HAVE.

...

THAT KNIFE...IS PRETTY MUCH MY LIFE.
G... GIVE IT BACK!

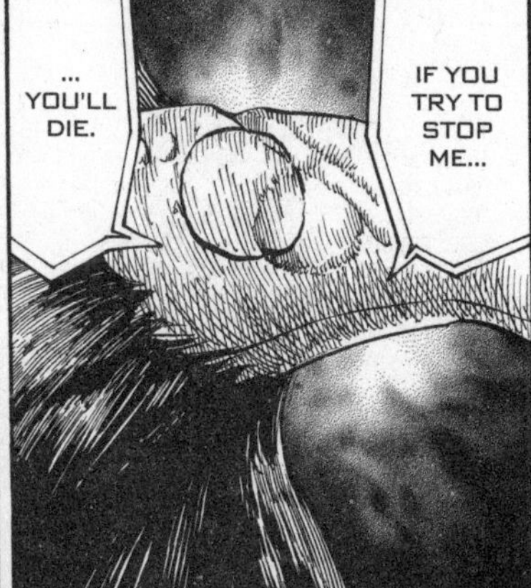
IF YOU TRY TO STOP ME...
...YOU'LL DIE.

I'M NOT AFRAID OF DYING!
I WROTE MY WILL BEFORE I CAME HERE!
NOW GIVE IT BACK!

!!!!
HUNH...
HIS RESOLVE IS REAL.
THAT'S RIGHT.
YOU'RE THE ONLY ONE...

YOU'RE THE ONLY COWARD HERE, GT ROBOT.

TORIKO ?!
TORIKO !!
BWAAAH
SHUF
SHUT OFF YOUR PRES-SURE SENSA-TION LIMIT.
I WANT YOU TO FEEL EVERY BLOW I DELIVER.
SHOW ME YOUR RESOLVE.
GOT IT?
...
HE ...
NO, IT CAN'T BE...

THIS IS WHAT HAPPENS WHEN YOU TAKE A WALK ON THE WILD SIDE!
YOU RUN THE RISK OF DYING !!
SKF
SKF
HEY, GT ROBOT !!

IT'S CRYSTAL CLEAR.
HIS CELLS HAVE EVOLVED.

HE MUST HAVE TASTED THE JEWEL MEAT!!

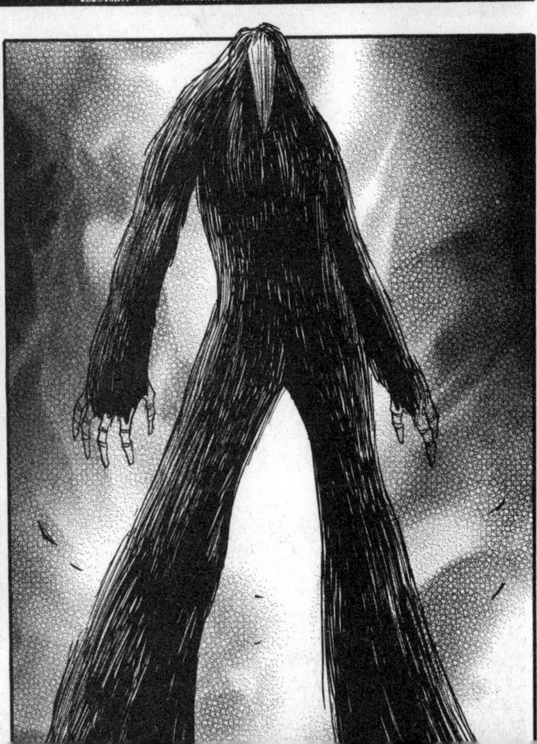

CONSIDER MY INTEREST PIQUED.

WHAT'S YOUR NAME?
DUM
DA

AS FAR AS I'M CON-CERNED, THESE GT ROBOTS ONLY HOLD ME BACK.

I'D PREFER GOING WITH-OUT THE PRES-SURE SENSA-TION LIMITS IN PLACE.

TORIKO...

THAT WAY I CAN CALCU-LATE...

...YOUR NEW STRENGTH MORE ACCU-RATELY.

OH, REALLY?

IN THAT CASE...

BETTER MAKE SURE THERE'S NO ROOM FOR REGRETS.

WHOOM
VOOSH
WHOA!

RRRRMMM
TEN-FOLD...
!!

TORIKO

GOURMET CHECKLIST

Vol. 036

DEATH GORE
(MAMMAL)

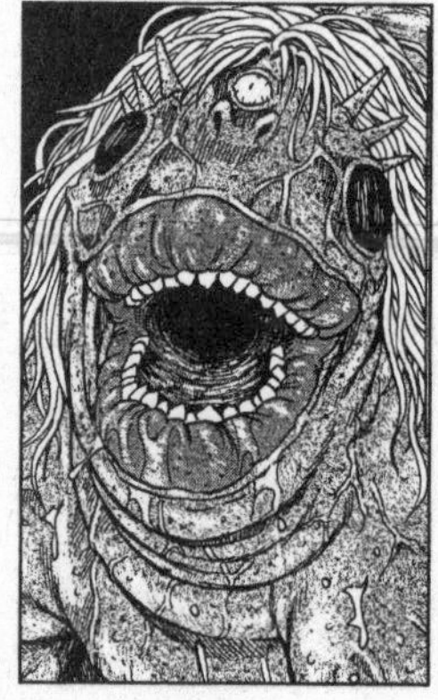

CAPTURE LEVEL: UNDETERMINED

HABITAT: FORESTS

LENGTH: 50 METERS

HEIGHT: ---

WEIGHT: 1,000~20,000 TONS

PRICE: UNKNOWN

SCALE

A MASSIVE HERBIVORE SAID TO HAVE LIVED MANY EONS AGO. THE DEATH GORE PICKED ITS TEETH WITH THE REMAINS OF THE FORESTS IT CONSUMED. SO VORACIOUS WAS THE SPECIES THAT IT REDUCED ALL THE WORLD'S WOODLANDS INTO DESERTS. THE ENTIRE RACE WAS MURDERED AT THE HANDS OF A YOUNG BATTLE WOLF, WHOSE TERRITORY THEY PASSED INTO. OR SO IT IS TOLD. AT THE VERY LEAST, IT IS THE OLDEST OF ALL THE IGO HISTORICAL SOCIETY'S DOCUMENTED FOOD CRISES.

PHEWWWN
RRRRRR
POP
POP
TEN-FOLD...
GOURMET 52: TEN-FOLD!!

MIXER
...
THUD
VRRRR---
--RR

IT STOPPED.
MY MIXER GOT JAMMED BY HIS STOMACH MUSCLES?!
YANK

HNN
...
VOOO
NG
KNIFE
!!!
!!
KRA
A A K K
YAH!
THAT
...
... WAS SO LOUD!
UNGH
...
BZZT
BZZT
OHH
!!

KNIF !!
KNIFE !!
KNIFE !!
HNGH ...
UUH ...
KNIIIFE !!!!

GASP...
PWAP
FORK!!!
WHOOSH
!

...OOH.
BZZZT
BZZZT
YAAAARGH!
STAB STAB STAB
STAB
STAB
STAB STAB
FOOORK!!!!
SKDDD

PSSHHH
GUH... HNGH!
KTANG
...
RARGH
PEELER...
FIVE-FOLD!!
B-B-B-B-BDUM
SPIKED PUNCH!!
B-B-B-B-BDUM
!!

KCAK KCAK
KCAK KCAK
KCAK KCAK
KCAK KCAK
KCAK
KCAK KCAK
SCHAAAP
NWWARRRGH!!

BZZT
BZZT

I SEE
BZZT
BZZT
SO THIS IS IT.

DID THE JEWEL MEAT TASTE GOOD?
TELL ME, TORIKO.

...
I WISHED TO TASTE IT MYSELF.
HEH HEH... OH, WELL.
I'LL HAVE THE JEWEL MEAT FOR MYSELF SOMEDAY.

WE SHALL MEET AGAIN, TORIKO.
NEXT TIME, IN PERSON.

DAMN STRAIGHT.
TEN-FOLD...

SPIKED PUNCH!!

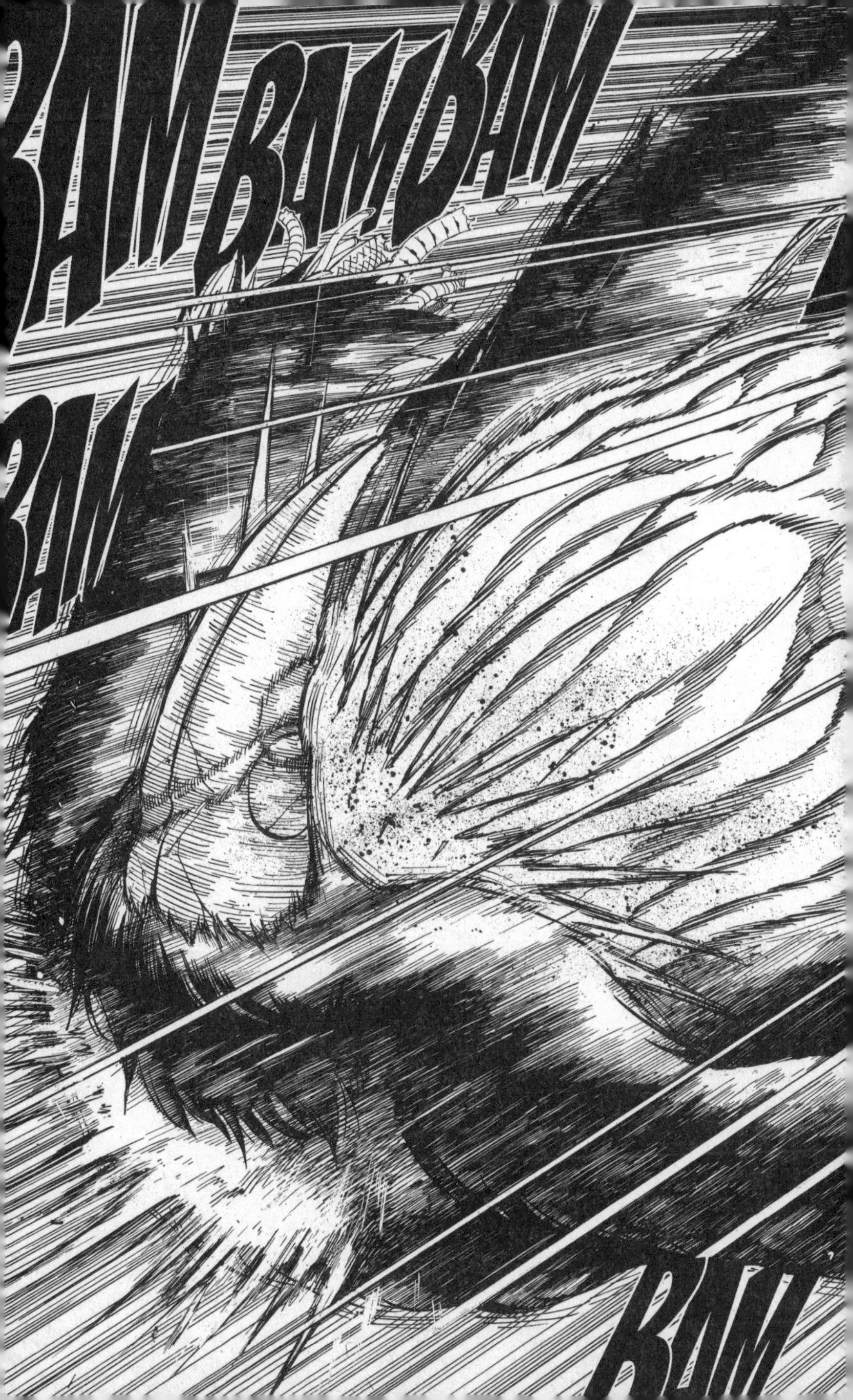
BAM
BAM
BAM
BAM
BAM

ZING
BRRK
KRIK

PA-POW
OOOO
BOOM
POW
NNSHT
KRIK

PWAM
PWAM
RIP
BZZT
SNAP
TING
TING
KRKL
BOOF
CHING
ST---

THANK YOU FOR THIS EXCEL-LENT MEAL.
TO BE CONTINUED!

BOOOOOO

TORIKO

GOURMET CHECKLIST

Vol. 037

HAYAN PANTHER

(MAMMAL)

CAPTURE LEVEL: 35 (RICKY)

HABITAT: IGO GOURMET LAB (NO DETAILS IN THE WILD)

LENGTH: 33 METERS

HEIGHT: 10 METERS

WEIGHT: 8 TONS

PRICE: UNKNOWN

SCALE

THE POSTER CHILD FOR THIS ANIMAL, RICKY, SERVES AS MANSOM'S PARTNER, AND WAS BRED IN THE IGO GOURMET LAB. HAYAN PANTHERS BOAST SUPERIOR ALERTNESS AND AGILITY PARTICULAR TO BIG CATS, AND THEIR SPEED IS SAID TO EXCEED THAT OF ANY OTHER MAMMAL'S (PUTTING IT UP THERE WITH THE BATTLE WOLF). THE WINGS ON ITS BACK ENABLE IT TO FLY SHORT DISTANCES, AND ALSO AID IN CUTTING DOWN WIND RESISTANCE WHEN THE PANTHER IS RUNNING. ON A DIFFERENT NOTE, RICKY'S FAVORITE FOOD IS GLOBBY PARFAIT, AND HE ALWAYS LOOKS FORWARD TO MANSOM REWARDING HIM WITH ONE.

CHARACTER PROFILE

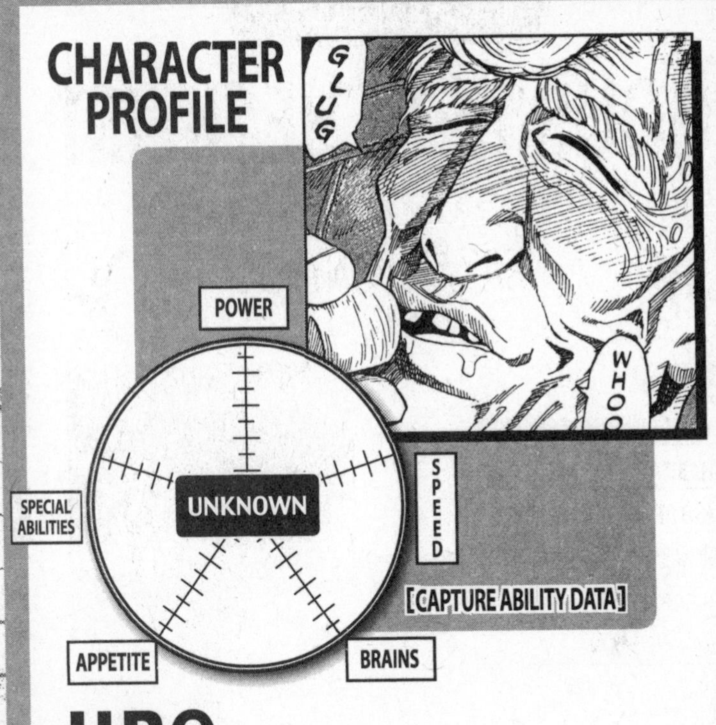

JIRO

AGE	UNKNOWN	BIRTHDAY:	FEBRUARY 2
BLOOD TYPE	B	SIGN:	AQUARIUS
HEIGHT	UNKNOWN	WEIGHT:	UNKNOWN
EYESIGHT	UNKNOWN	SHOE SIZE:	UNKNOWN

SPECIAL MOVES/ABILITIES

- **UNKOWN**

A Gourmet Hunter who has earned the nickname "The Knocking Master." He's supposedly retired, but will sometimes go on a hunt for the fun of it. This character is a riddle wrapped in an enigma, and that goes for just what he's capable of too.

CHARACTER PROFILE

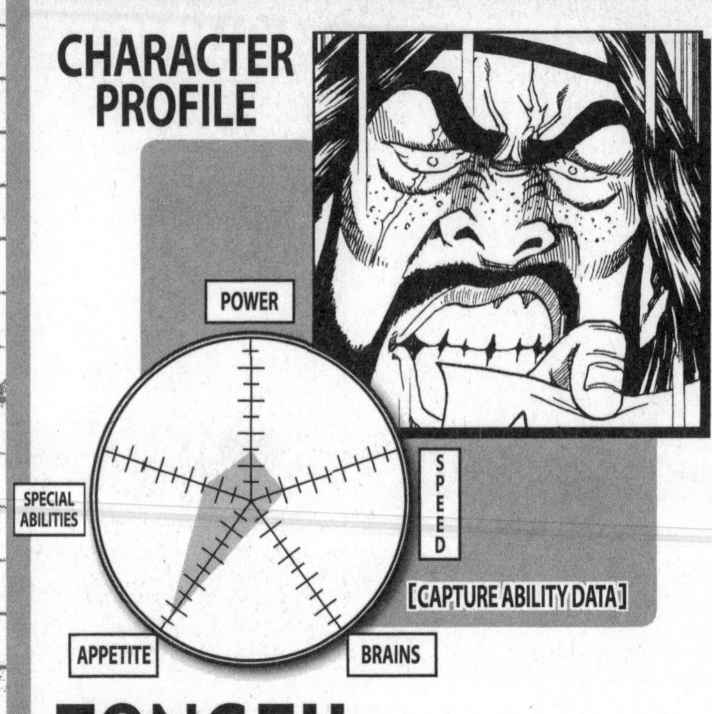

ZONGEH

AGE	27	BIRTHDAY:	JULY 8
BLOOD TYPE	B	SIGN:	CANCER
HEIGHT	182 CM	WEIGHT:	100 KG
EYESIGHT	10/20	SHOE SIZE:	28 CM

SPECIAL MOVES/ABILITIES

- **Zongeh Rush (just swinging his ax around)**
  Zongeh Mash (hitting an enemy with his ax)

Self-proclaimed Gourmet Hunter. He tries to come off as a big drinker and will guzzle vodka and such for show, but deep down he's a sucker for sweet drinks like Kahlua Milk. Despite his limitations, he's pretty passionate and commands trust and respect from his men.

COMING NEXT VOLUME

CORN FIT FOR A KING

Having finally succeeded in capturing the delicious Jewel Meat, Toriko and friends celebrate with a mega feast. However, something seems wrong with Terry's appetite. In order to find a suitable meal for this picky battle wolf, Toriko will travel deep into a dangerous jungle to locate the legendary BB corn!

AVAILABLE NOW!

DEMON SLAYER

KIMETSU NO YAIBA

Story and Art by

KOYOHARU GOTOUGE

In Taisho-era Japan, kindhearted Tanjiro Kamado makes a living selling charcoal. But his peaceful life is shattered when a demon slaughters his entire family. His little sister Nezuko is the only survivor, but she has been transformed into a demon herself! Tanjiro sets out on a dangerous journey to find a way to return his sister to normal and destroy the demon who ruined his life.

Story and Art by
KOYOHARU
GOTOUGE

AKIRA TORIYAMA

DRAGON QUEST

ILLUSTRATIONS

Akira Toriyama (*Dragon Ball*) brought the world of the renowned *Dragon Quest* video games to life through his creative, fun and inventive design work. Thirty years of genius are on display in this stunningly comprehensive hardcover collection of over 500 illustrations from the *Dragon Quest* video games. Includes fold-out poster of the *Dragon Quest* timeline.

You're Reading in the Wrong Direction!!

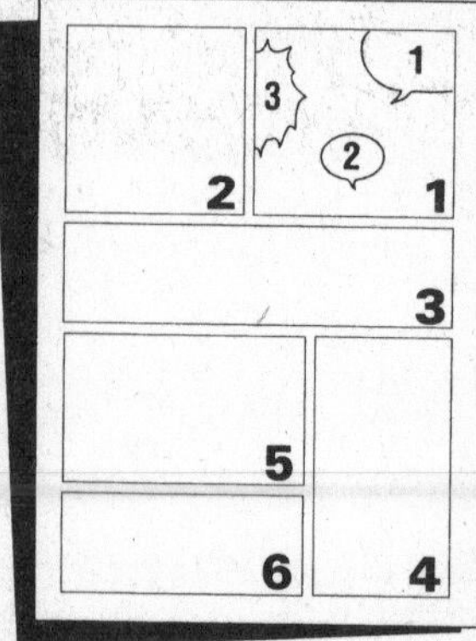

Whoops! Guess what? You're starting at the wrong end of the comic! ...It's true! In keeping with the original Japanese format, **Toriko** is meant to be read from right to left, starting in the upper-right corner.

Unlike English, which is read from left to right, Japanese is read from right to left, meaning that action, sound effects and word-balloon order are completely reversed... something which can make readers unfamiliar with Japanese feel pretty backwards themselves. For this reason, manga or Japanese comics published in the U.S. in English have sometimes been published "flopped"—that is, printed in exact reverse order, as though seen from the other side of a mirror.

By flopping pages, U.S. publishers can avoid confusing readers, but the compromise is not without its downside. For one thing, a character in a flopped manga series who once wore in the original Japanese version a T-shirt emblazoned with "M A Y" (as in "the merry month of") now wears one which reads "Y A M"! Additionally, many manga creators in Japan are themselves unhappy with the process, as some feel the mirror-imaging of their art skews their original intentions.

We are proud to bring you Mitsutoshi Shimabukuro's **Toriko** in the original unflopped format. For now, though, turn to the other side of the book and let the adventure begin...!

—Editor